TREASURED THOUGHTS

Treasured Thoughts
For Today, Tomorrow and Always

Hallmark Editions   Illustrated by James R. Hamil and Asterio Pascolini

Acknowledgments: Excerpt from "Sheer Joy" in *Spiritual Hilltops* by Ralph Cushman. Used by permission of Abingdon Press. "At Day's End" from *The Gypsy Heart* by Emily Carey Alleman. Copyright 1957 by Emily Carey Alleman. Used by arrangement. Ecclesiastes 3:1-8; Proverbs 15:13; 31:10, 25-31; Leviticus 19:18; Philippians 4:11; Psalm 46:10; I Thessalonians 5:18; Genesis 21:6; Numbers 6:24-26; and James 3:17 from the *King James Version Bible*. Reprinted by permission of the Cambridge University Press. Published by the Syndics of Cambridge University Press. Excerpt by Pablo Picasso (NBC-TV September 15, 1957) in *Contemporary Quotations*, compiled by James B. Simpson. Copyright © 1964 by James B. Simpson. Used with permission of Thomas Y. Crowell Company, Inc. Excerpt from "Nature Lover's Creed" by Thomas Curtis Clark. Used by permission. Excerpt by Adelaide Love reprinted by permission of Dodd, Mead & Company, Incorporated from *The Slender Singing Tree* by Adelaide Love. Copyright © 1933, 1961 by Adelaide Love. "Loving-kindness…" by W. Somerset Maugham from *The Summing Up*. Copyright 1938 by W. Somerset Maugham. Reprinted by permission of Doubleday & Company, Inc. Haiku by Taigi, Basho and Shiki from *Silent Flowers*, edited by Dorothy Price. Copyright © 1967 by Hallmark Cards, Inc. and Hokuseido Press. Used by arrangement. Excerpt "One watches people starting out in life quite adequately…" from *On Being a Real Person* by Harry Emerson Fosdick, copyright 1943, Harper & Row, Publishers, Inc. Used by permission of the publishers and SCM Press, London. "I Never Saw a Moor" reprinted by permission of the publishers and the Trustees of Amherst College from Thomas H. Johnson, Editor, *The Poems of Emily Dickinson*, Cambridge, Mass.: The Belknap Press of Harvard University Press, Copyright, 1951, 1955, by the President and Fellows of Harvard College. "Youth's Dream of Beauty" reprinted by permission of Hawthorn Books, Inc., from *Messer Marco Polo* by Donn Byrne. Copyright © 1921 by Appleton-Century-Crofts. All Rights Reserved. "Stopping by Woods on a Snowy Evening" from *The Poetry of Robert Frost* edited by Edward Connery Lathem. Copyright 1923, © 1969 by Holt, Rinehart and Winston, Inc. Copyright 1951 by Robert Frost. Reprinted by permission of Holt, Rinehart and Winston, Inc. and the Estate of Robert Frost and Jonathan Cape Limited as publishers. "High Flight" by John Gillespie Magee, Jr., from *New York Herald Tribune*. Used by permission of I.H.T. Corporation. Excerpts by Kahlil Gibran reprinted from *The Prophet* by Kahlil Gibran, with permission of the publisher, Alfred A. Knopf, Inc. Copyright 1923 by Kahlil Gibran: renewal copyright 1951 by Administrators C. T. A. of Kahlil Gibran Estate, and Mary G. Gibran. "We Thank Thee" by James Keller. Used by permission of the author. Verses by John V. A. Weaver from *In American* by John V. A. Weaver. Copyright 1921 by Alfred A. Knopf, Inc., and renewed 1949 by Margaret Wood Walling. Reprinted by permission of the publisher. Excerpt by Emily Dickinson from *Selected Poems and Letters of Emily Dickinson*, edited by Robert N. Linscott. Copyright © 1959 by Robert N. Linscott. Used by permission of Elisabeth Linscott, Trustee. "Sea Fever" and "Laugh and Be Merry" from *Poems* by John Masefield. Copyright 1912 by Macmillan Publishing Co., Inc., renewed 1940 by John Masefield. Reprinted with permission of Macmillan Publishing Co., Inc., and The Society of Authors as the Literary representative of the Estate of John Masefield. "Man's Heritage of Courage" reprinted with permission of Macmillan Publishing Company, Inc., from *You Can Master Life* by James Gordon Gilkey. Copyright 1934 by Macmillan Publishing Company, Inc., renewed 1962 by James Gordon Gilkey. "Needed: Good Samaritans" from *The Philosophy of Civilization* by Albert Schweitzer, published in the United States by Macmillan Publishing Co., Inc., 1949. Used by permission of Macmillan Publishing Co., Inc., and A. C. Black, Ltd. "There are hermit souls that live withdrawn…" from "The House by the Side of the Road" from *Dreams in Homespun* by Sam Walter Foss. (Lothrop, Lee & Shepard.) Reprinted with permission of William Morrow & Company, Inc. Daniel 2:20, 23 from the *Revised Standard Version Bible*. Reprinted by permission of the National Council of the Churches of Christ. Ecclesiasticus 6:14-17 from the *Revised Standard Version Bible — Catholic Edition*. Used by arrangement. Excerpt "This is the miracle that happens…" reprinted from *Letters of Rainer Maria Rilke, 1892-1910*. Translated by Jane Bannard Greene and M. D. Herter Norton. Used by permission of W. W. Norton & Company, Inc. "Twilight's Feet" by Agnes T. Pratt. Used by permission of the author, former student, Institute of American Indian Arts, a Bureau of Indian Affairs school. "Beauty" from *From a College Window* by A. C. Benson. Reprinted by permission of G. P. Putnam's Sons. "Care-Free Youth," "Peace," "Life," "Gratitude," "A Toast to Happiness," "Faith," "Courage," "Home," "My Creed" from *A Heap o' Livin'* by Edgar A. Guest, copyright 1916, 1944 Reilly and Lee Company. All by permission of Henry Regnery Company. "Beauty" from *Mr. Jones, Meet the Master* by Peter Marshall. Copyright © 1949, 1950 by Fleming H. Revell Company. Reprinted by permission. "Little Boy Blue" by Eugene Field from *The Poetical Works of Eugene Field* used by permission of Charles Scribner's Sons. Verse by George Santayana from "A Minuet on Reaching the Age of Fifty" (Copyright 1923 Charles Scribner's Sons) by George Santayana from *Poems* is reprinted with permission of Charles Scribner's Sons and Constable & Co., Ltd. "The Art of Hope" from *More About the Art of Living* by Wilferd A. Peterson. Copyright © 1966 by Wilferd A. Peterson. Used by permission of Simon & Schuster, Inc. Excerpt by Robert Beverly Hale reprinted by permission from *Time*, The Weekly Newsmagazine; Copyright 1960 Time Inc. "The Mystery of Life" from *The Log From the Sea of Cortez* by John Steinbeck. Copyright 1951 by John Steinbeck. Copyright 1941 by John Steinbeck and Edward F. Ricketts. Copyright © renewed 1969 by John Steinbeck and Edward F. Ricketts, Jr. All Rights Reserved. Reprinted by permission of The Viking Press and McIntosh and Otis, Inc. "Trees" by Joyce Kilmer. Copyright 1913 and renewed 1941. Copyright assigned to Jerry Vogel Music Company, Inc. Used by permission of Jerry Vogel Music Company. "The fruit of the spirit is…joy." From *Words Are No Good if the Game Is Solitaire* by Herbert B. Barks. Copyright 1971 by Word, Inc. Used by permission. "My Love" by Eileen Perlman from *Timeless Treasures*, selected by Jeanne Hollyfield, designed and produced by Young Publications. Copyright 1966 by Lincoln B. Young. Used by permission. Excerpt by Lin Yutang from *On the Wisdom of America* by Lin Yutang, copyright 1950 by The John Day Company. Used by permission of the author.

Editorial Research: Katherine Hollingshead
Editorial Direction: Aileene Neighbors
Design: Rick Cusick
Production Art: Joyce Bishop

Copyright © 1974 by Hallmark Cards, Inc., Kansas City, Missouri. All Rights Reserved. Printed in the United States of America.
Library of Congress Catalog Card Number: 74-75312. Standard Book Number: 87529-389-1.

TREASURED THOUGHTS

An Invitation

Welcome to a timeless celebration of the written word. *Treasured Thoughts* is a beautiful collection of superior writing that invites each reader to experience such emotions as the comforts of friendship, the blessings of contentment, the exuberance of youth, the beauties of age and the wonderful mysteries of life itself.

Whether you're reflecting on thoughts of the past or savoring messages of the present, these inspired pages are sure to warm your heart and fill your spirit with joy.

Sensitive illustrations, beautiful lettering and superb craftsmanship all combine to make this unique collection a keepsake of inspiration that you, your family and friends will truly enjoy today, tomorrow and always.

Contents

PEACE 11 Peace is happiness digesting.
Victor Hugo

HAPPINESS 15 I had a pleasant time with my mind, for it was happy.
Louisa May Alcott

FRIENDSHIP 19 A true friend is the best possession.
Benjamin Franklin

FAITH 23 Faith is the antiseptic of the soul.
Walt Whitman

COURAGE 27 The things courage can do!
Sir James M. Barrie

TRUTH 31 Truth is beautiful.
Ralph Waldo Emerson

BROTHERHOOD 35 If God is thy father, man is thy brother.
Alphonse de Lamartine

BELIEF 39 Man is what he believes.
Anton Chekhov

BEAUTY 43 Beauty is eternity gazing at itself in a mirror.
Kahlil Gibran

Contents

ART   49   Art is man added to nature.
                  Francis Bacon

GOD   53   The first of all beautiful things is the continual possession of God.
                  Saint Gregory Nazianzen

HOPE   57   Hope is the dream of a man awake.
                  Matthew Prior

HOME   61   There is no place more delightful than home.
                  Cicero

SEASONS   67   The seasons come and go, and go and come, to teach men gratitude.
                  Robert Pollok

PRAYER   71   Prayer is the world in tune.
                  Henry Vaughan

LIFE   75   Every man's life is a fairy tale, written by God's fingers.
                  Hans Christian Andersen

KINDNESS   81   Paradise is open to all kind hearts.
                  Pierre Jean de Béranger

NATURE   83   Nature is visible thought.
                  Heinrich Heine

Contents

YOUTH   89   The thoughts of youth are long, long thoughts.
Henry Wadsworth Longfellow

LAUGHTER   93   A day is wasted without laughter.
Nicolas Chamfort

AGE   95   The autumn of the beautiful is beautiful.
Latin Proverb

MOTHERHOOD   99   Where there is a mother in the house, matters speed well.
Amos Bronson Alcott

MEMORIES   105   The true art of memory is the art of attention.
Samuel Johnson

IMAGINATION   107   Imagination is the eye of the soul.
Joseph Joubert

LOVE   111   Love comforteth like sunshine after rain.
William Shakespeare

CONTENTMENT   115   A contented mind is the greatest blessing a man can enjoy in this world.
Joseph Addison

GRATITUDE   119   Gratitude is the memory of the heart.
Jean Baptiste Massieu

Peace

Compensation

The mountain wears a mellow mood today,
A haze of transient glory crowns its crest,
Where purpling blues and pinks hold
    cloudless sway
As evening banks long sunbeams
    in the west.
He who turns his face to peaceful hills
Has drunk the cup of Life that Beauty spills.
    Mary Beale Carr

PEACE

One watches people starting out in life quite adequately, handling life with active vigor, as they run, one after another, into experiences where something deeper than vigor is needed. Serious failure, for example. Some night in his lifetime everyone comes home to find a new guest there--disappointment. What he had set his heart on has gone....If one is to come through difficult experiences unembittered, unspoiled, still a real person, one needs deep resources....Not alone in such experiences as sorrow and failure does this need arise but in man's search for the indispensable spiritual requirements of a satisfying life--inner peace, for example, some serenity in the soul to come home to at night and go out from in the morning. Who does not need that? But no one can get inner peace by pouncing on it, by vigorously willing to have it. Peace is a margin of power around our daily need. Peace is a consciousness of springs too deep for earthly droughts to dry up. Peace is an awareness of reserves from beyond ourselves, so that our power is not so much in us as through us.
Harry Emerson Fosdick

Make peace with yourself, and heaven and earth will make peace with you. Endeavor to enter into your own inner cell, and you will see the heavens; because the one and the other are one and the same, and when you enter one you see the two.
Saint Isaak of Syria

If there is righteousness in the heart, there will be beauty in character. If there is beauty in character, there will be harmony in the home. If there is harmony in the home, there will be order in the nation. If there is order in the nation, there will be peace in the world.
A Chinese Proverb

Peace is happiness digesting.

VICTOR HUGO

Peace

With eager heart and will on fire,
I fought to win my great desire
"Peace shall be mine," I said; but life
Grew bitter in the weary strife.

My soul was tired, and my pride
Was wounded deep: to Heaven I cried,
"God grant me peace or I must die;"
The dumb stars glittered no reply.

Broken at last, I bowed my head,
Forgetting all myself, and said,
"Whatever comes, His will be done;"
And in that moment peace was won.
Henry van Dyke

Speak, move, act in peace, as if you were in prayer. In truth, this is prayer.
Francis de S. Fenelon

Peace is the golden wisp that binds the sheaf of blessings.
Katharine Lee Bates

Peace is the evening star of the soul, as virtue is its sun; and the two are never far apart.
Colton

The Lord bless thee, and keep thee:
The Lord make his face shine upon thee,
　and be gracious unto thee:
The Lord lift up his countenance upon thee,
　and give thee peace.
Numbers 6:24-26

How beautiful upon the mountains,
　How beautiful upon the downs,
　How beautiful in the village post office,
　On the pavements of towns--
How beautiful in the huge print
　　of newspapers,
Beautiful while telegraph wires hum,
While telephone bells wildly jingle,
The news that peace has come--
That peace has come at last--
　that all wars cease.
How beautiful upon the mountains
　are the footsteps
Of the messengers of peace!
Alice Duer Miller

But the wisdom that is from above is first pure, then peaceable, gentle, and easy to be intreated, full of mercy and good fruits, without partiality, and without hypocrisy.
James 3:17

Peace

A man must earn his hour of peace,
　Must pay for it with hours of strife and care,
Must win by toil the evening's sweet release,
　The rest that may be portioned for his share;
The idler never knows it, never can.
　Peace is the glory ever of a man.

A man must win contentment for his soul,
　Must battle for it bravely day by day;
The peace he seeks is not a nearby goal;
　To claim it he must tread a rugged way.
The shirker never knows a tranquil breast;
　Peace but rewards the man who does his best.
Edgar A. Guest

Happiness

Sea Fever

I must go down to the seas again,
   to the lonely sea and the sky,
And all I ask is a tall ship
   and a star to steer her by;
And the wheel's kick and the wind's song
   and the white sail's shaking,
And a grey mist on the sea's face,
   and a grey dawn breaking.

I must go down to the seas again,
   for the call of the running tide
Is a wild call and a clear call
   that may not be denied;
And all I ask is a windy day
   with the white clouds flying,
And the flung spray and the blown spume,
   and the sea-gulls crying.

I must go down to the seas again,
   to the vagrant gypsy life,
To the gull's way and the whale's way,
   where the wind's like a whetted knife;
And all I ask is a merry yarn
   from a laughing fellow-rover,
And quiet sleep and a sweet dream
   when the long trick's over.

John Masefield

True happiness is to understand our duties toward God and man, to enjoy the present without anxious dependence upon the future, not to amuse ourselves with either hopes or fears, but to rest satisfied with what we have, which is abundantly sufficient; for he that is so wants nothing. The great blessings of mankind are within us, and within our reach; but we shut our eyes and, like people in the dark, fall foul of the very thing we search for without finding it. Tranquillity is a certain equality of mind which no condition of fortune can either exalt or depress.

There must be sound mind to make a happy man; there must be constancy in all conditions, a care for the things of this world but without anxiety; and such an indifference to the bounties of fortune that either with them or without them we may live content. True joy is serene....The seat of it is within, and there is no cheerfulness like the resolution of a brave mind that has fortune under its feet. It is an invincible greatness of mind not to be elevated or dejected with good or ill fortune. A wise man is content with his lot, whatever it be--without wishing for what he has not.

Seneca

The Joy of Doing
The secret of happiness is in knowing this: that we live by the law of expenditure. We find greatest joy, not in getting, but in expressing what we are. There are tides in the ocean of life, and what comes in depends on what goes out. The currents flow inward only where there is an outlet. Nature does not give to those who will not spend; her gifts are loaned to those who will use them. Empty your lungs and breathe. Run, climb, work, and laugh; the more you give out, the more you shall receive. Be exhausted, and you shall be fed. Men do not really live for honors or for pay; their gladness is not in the taking and holding, but in the doing, the striving, the building, the living. It is a higher joy to teach than to be taught. It is good to get justice, but better to do it; fun to have things but more to make them. The happy man is he who lives the life of love, not for the honors it may bring, but for the life itself.

R. J. Baughan

The fruit of the spirit is...joy.
I have only the faintest hint as to what joy is. I know we could not stand much of it at one time.
Perhaps, it is the few times in our life when we know we are being
    who we should be
    when we should be
    where we should be.
"Joy." It is the most magical, haunting image I know.

Herbert B. Barks

Three grand essentials to happiness in this life are something to do, something to love and something to hope for.
Joseph Addison

All who joy would win
Must share it,--happiness was born a twin.
George Gordon, Lord Byron

Happiness is essentially a state of going somewhere wholeheartedly.
W. H. Sheldon

Our home joys are the most delightful earth affords, and the joy of parents in their children is the most holy joy of humanity. It makes their hearts pure and good; it lifts men up to their Father in heaven.
Johann Heinrich Pestalozzi

Happiness and virtue rest upon each other; the best are not only the happiest, but the happiest are usually the best.
Edward Bulwer-Lytton

The world would be better and brighter if our teachers would dwell on the Duty of Happiness as well as the Happiness of Duty, for we ought to be as cheerful as we can, if only because to be happy ourselves is a most effectual contribution to the happiness of others.
Sir John Lubbock

Happiness is a butterfly, which, when pursued, is always just beyond your grasp, but which, if you will sit down quietly, may alight upon you.
Nathaniel Hawthorne

Happiness is like coke--something you get as a by-product in the process of making something else.
Aldous Huxley

A merry heart maketh a cheerful countenance.
Proverbs 15:13

I had a pleasant time with my mind, for it was happy.
Louisa May Alcott

Happiness depends, as Nature shows,
Less on exterior things than most suppose.
William Cowper

He is the happiest man who can connect the end of his life with its beginning.
Wolfgang von Goethe

from Sheer Joy
Oh the sheer joy of it!
Walking with thee,
Out on the hilltop,
Down by the sea,
Life is so wonderful,
Life is so free.

Oh the sheer joy of it!
Working with God,
Running His errands,
Waiting His nod,
Building His heaven,
On common sod.
Ralph Spaulding Cushman

A Toast to Happiness

To happiness I raise my glass,
    The goal of every human,
The hope of every clan and class
    And every man and woman.
The daydreams of the urchin there,
The sweet theme of the maiden's prayer,
    The strong man's one ambition,
The sacred prize of mothers sweet,
The tramp of soldiers on the street
    Have all the selfsame mission.
Life here is nothing more nor less
Than just a quest for happiness.

Some seek it on the mountain top,
    And some within a mine;
The widow in her notion shop
    Expects its sun to shine.
The tramp that seeks new roads to fare
Is one with king and millionaire
    In this that each is groping
On different roads, in different ways,
To come to glad, contented days,
    And shares the common hoping.
The sound of martial fife and drum
Is born of happiness to come.

Yet happiness is always here
    Had we the eyes to see it;
No breast but holds a fund of cheer
    Had man the will to free it.
'Tis there upon the mountain top,
Or in the widow's notion shop,
    'Tis found in homes of sorrow;
'Tis woven in the memories
Of happier, brighter days than these,
    The gift, not of to-morrow
But of to-day, and in our tears
Some touch of happiness appears.

'Tis not a joy that's born of wealth:
    The poor man may possess it.
'Tis not alone the prize of health:
    No sickness can repress it.
'Tis not the end of mortal strife,
The sunset of the day of life,
    Or but the old should find it;
It is the bond twixt God and man,
The touch divine in all we plan,
    And has the soul behind it.
And so this toast to happiness,
The seed of which we all possess.
Edgar A. Guest

It is the chiefest point of happiness that a man is willing to be what he is.
Erasmus

I wish you all the joy that you can wish.
William Shakespeare

Friendship

Friendship

Oh, the comfort--the inexpressible
  comfort of feeling safe with a person,
Having neither to weigh thoughts,
Nor measure words--but pouring them
All right out--just as they are--
Chaff and grain together--
Certain that a faithful hand will
Take and sift them--
Keep what is worth keeping--
And with the breath of kindness
Blow the rest away.

Dinah Maria Mulock Craik

A friend is the first person who comes in when the whole world has gone out.
W. R. Alger

What is a friend? A single soul dwelling in two bodies.
Aristotle

The best mirror is an old friend.
George Herbert

When the way is long, company is pleasant.
from the Talmud

Of all the things which wisdom provides to make life entirely happy, much the greatest is the possession of friendship.
Epicurus

Nothing can be sweeter than friendship.
Petrarch

Friends should be like books, easy to find when you need them, but seldom used.
Ralph Waldo Emerson

Friendship
A ruddy drop of manly blood
The surging sea outweighs,
The world uncertain comes and goes;
The lover rooted stays.
I fancied he was fled,
And, after many a year,
Glowed unexhausted kindliness,
Like daily sunrise there.
My careful heart was free again,
O friend, my bosom said,
Through thee alone the sky is arched,
Through thee the rose is red;
All things through thee take nobler form,
And look beyond the earth,
The mill-round of our fate appears
A sun-path in thy worth.
Me too thy nobleness has taught
To master my despair;
The fountains of my hidden life
Are through thy friendship fair.
Ralph Waldo Emerson

Friendship is the only cement that will hold the world together.
Woodrow Wilson

Just a Thought
O the miles that stretch between us
 Just seem longer every day;
May you find a joy in knowing
 That you're just a thought away.
Many miles may separate us
 And the clouds between be gray,
But you're cherished in my heart, dear,
 And you're just a thought away.
Glenna Hull

Friendship is the shadow of the evening, which strengthens with the setting sun of life.
Jean de La Fontaine

The happiest moments of my life have been in the flow of affection among friends.
Thomas Jefferson

Friendship is the positive and unalterable choice of a person whom we have singled out for qualities that we most admire.
Abel Bonnard

*A true friend
is the best possession.*

BENJAMIN FRANKLIN

Now friendship is nothing else than a complete union of feeling on all subjects, divine and human, accompanied by kindly feeling and attachment; than which, indeed, I am not aware whether, with the exception of wisdom, anything better has been bestowed on man by the immortal gods.
Cicero

Blessed are they who have the gift of making friends, for it is one of God's best gifts. It involves many things, but above all, the power of going out of one's self and appreciating whatever is noble and loving in another.
Thomas Hughes

Little Boy Blue
The little toy dog is covered with dust,
    But sturdy and stanch he stands;
And the little toy soldier is red with rust,
    And his musket molds in his hands.
Time was when the little toy dog was new
    And the soldier was passing fair,
And that was the time when our Little Boy Blue
    Kissed them and put them there.

"Now, don't you go till I come," he said,
    "And don't you make any noise!"
So toddling off to his trundle-bed
    He dreamed of the pretty toys.
And as he was dreaming, an angel song
    Awakened our Little Boy Blue--
Oh, the years are many, the years are long,
    But the little toy friends are true.

Ay, faithful to Little Boy Blue they stand,
    Each in the same old place,
Awaiting the touch of a little hand,
    And the smile of a little face.
And they wonder, as waiting these long years through,
    In the dust of that little chair,
What has become of our Little Boy Blue
    Since he kissed them and put them there.
Eugene Field

A faithful friend is a strong defense: and he that hath found him hath found a treasure.

Nothing can be compared to a faithful friend: and no weight of gold and silver is able to countervail the goodness of his fidelity.

A faithful friend is the medicine of life and immortality: and they that fear the Lord shall find him.

He that feareth God shall likewise have good friendship: because according to him shall his friend be.

Ecclesiasticus 6:14-17

Friends, those relations that one makes for one's self.

Deschamps

God gives us our relatives; thank God we can choose our friends.

Addison Mizner

May the hinges of friendship never rust, or the wings of love lose a feather.

Anonymous

A friend is a person who knows all about you--and still likes you.

Elbert Hubbard

The Comfort of Friends
They, that love beyond the world cannot be separated by it.

Death cannot kill what never dies.

Nor can spirits ever be divided that love and live in the same divine principle; the root and record of their friendship.

If absence be not death, neither is theirs.

Death is but crossing the world, as friends do the seas; they live in one another still.

For they must needs be present, that love and live in that which is Omnipresent.

In this divine glass they see face to face; and their converse is free as well as pure.

This is the comfort of friends, that though they may be said to die, yet their friendship and society are, in the best sense, ever present, because immortal.

William Penn

Friendship hath the skill and observation of the best physician, the diligence and vigilance of the best nurse, and the tenderness and patience of the best mother.

Edward Hyde

You're my friend--
What a thing friendship is, world without end!
How it gives the heart and soul a stir-up.

Robert Browning

Faith

D ivine Love always has met and always will meet every human need.
Mary Baker Eddy

FAITH

Testament of Faith
You see I have some reason to wish that, in a future state, I may not only be as well as I was, but a little better. And I hope it; for I…trust in God. And when I observe that there is great frugality, as well as wisdom in His works, since He has been evidently sparing both of labor and materials; for by the various wonderful inventions of propagation He has provided for the continual peopling of His world with plants and animals, without being at the trouble of repeated new creations; and by the natural reduction of compound substances to their original elements, capable of being employed in new compositions, He has prevented the necessity of creating new matter; so that the earth, water, air and perhaps fire, which being compounded from wood, do, when the wood is dissolved return and again become air, earth, fire and water; I say that when I see nothing annihilated, and not even a drop of water wasted, I cannot suspect the annihilation of souls; or believe that He will suffer the daily waste of millions of minds ready made that now exist and put Himself to the continual trouble of making new ones. Thus finding myself to exist in the world, I believe I shall in some shape or other, always exist; and, with all the inconveniences human life is liable to, I shall not object to a new edition of mine; hoping, however, that the errata of the last may be corrected.
Benjamin Franklin
Letter to George Whatley, 1785

Where there is Faith,
There is Love.
Where there is Love,
There is Peace.
Where there is Peace,
There is God.
Where there is God,
There is no need.
ANONYMOUS

Heaven is not gained at a single bound;
But we build the ladder by which we rise
From the lowly earth to the vaulted skies,
And we mount to its summit, round
   by round.
J. G. Holland

For what is faith unless it is to believe
what you do not see?
Saint Augustine

I am always content with what happens for
I know that what God chooses is better than
what I choose.
Epictetus

To have faith is to have wings.
Sir James M. Barrie

Faith is the antiseptic of the soul.
Walt Whitman

I Never Saw a Moor
I never saw a Moor--
I never saw the Sea--
Yet know I how the Heather looks
And what a Billow be.

I never spoke with God
Nor visited in Heaven--
Yet certain am I of the spot
As if the Checks were given.
Emily Dickinson

The Voice of Faith
I have seen a curious child, who dwelt upon a tract
Of inland ground, applying to his ear
The convolutions of a smooth-lipped shell;
To which, in silence hushed, his very soul
Listened intensely; for from within were heard
Murmurings, whereby the monitor expressed
Mysterious union with its native sea.
Even such a shell the universe itself
Is to the ear of faith; and there are times,
I doubt not, when to you it doth impart
Authentic tidings of invisible things,
Of ebb and flow, and ever-enduring power,
And central peace, subsisting at the heart
Of endless agitation.
William Wordsworth

Be still, and know that I am God.
Psalm 46:10

Give me faith, Lord, and let me help others
to find it.
Leo Tolstoy

Faith is the soul riding at anchor.
Henry Wheeler Shaw

Faith

I believe in the world and its bigness and splendor;
That most of the hearts beating round us are tender;
That days are but footsteps and years are but miles
That lead us to beauty and singing and smiles:
That roses that blossom and toilers that plod
Are filled with the glorious spirit of God.

I believe in the purpose of everything living:
That taking is but the forerunner of giving;
That strangers are friends that we some day may meet;
And not all the bitter can equal the sweet;
That creeds are but colors, and no man has said
That God loves the yellow rose more than the red.

I believe in the path that to-day I am treading,
That I shall come safe through the dangers I'm dreading;
That even the scoffer shall turn from his ways
And some day be won back to trust and to praise;
That the leaf on the tree and the thing we call Man
Are sharing alike in His infinite plan.

I believe that all things that are living and breathing
Some richness of beauty to earth are bequeathing;
That all that goes out of this world leaves behind
Some duty accomplished for mortals to find;
That the humblest of creatures our praise is deserving,
For it, with the wisest, the Master is serving.

Edgar A. Guest

Faith Is Man's Heritage

Faith is a sentiment, for it is a hope; it is an instinct, for it precedes all outward instruction. Faith is the heritage of the individual at birth; it is that which binds him to the whole of being. The individual only detaches himself with difficulty from the maternal breast; he only isolates himself by an effort from the nature around him, from the love which enwraps him, the ideas in which he floats, the cradle in which he lies. He is born in union with humanity, with the world, and with God. The trace of this original union is faith....

    The need of faith never leaves us. It is the postulate of a higher truth which is to bring all things into harmony. It is the stimulus of research; it holds out to us the reward, it points us to the goal. Such at least is the true, the excellent faith.

Henri Frederic Amiel

When the Sun Bursts Forth

When mists have hung low over the hills, and the day has been dark with intermittent showers, at length great clouds begin to hurry across the sky, the wind rises, and the rain comes pouring down; then we look out and exclaim: "Why, this is the clearing-up shower." And when the floods have spent themselves, the clouds part to let the blue sky tremble through them, and the west wind bears them away seaward, and, though they are yet black and threatening, we see their silver edges as they pass and know that just behind them are singing birds and glittering dewdrops; and, lo! while yet we look, the sun bursts forth and lights them up in the eastern heaven with the glory of the rainbow.

Henry Ward Beecher

Courage

COURAGE

Concord Hymn
By the rude bridge that arched the flood,
Their flag to April's breeze unfurled,
Here once the embattled farmers stood
And fired the shot heard round the world.

The foe long since in silence slept;
Alike the conqueror silent sleeps;
And Time the ruined bridge has swept
Down the dark stream which seaward creeps.

On this green bank, by this soft stream,
We set today a votive stone;
That memory may their deed redeem,
When, like our sires, our sons are gone.

Spirit, that made those heroes dare
To die and leave their children free,
Bid Time and Nature gently spare
The shaft we raise to them and thee.
Ralph Waldo Emerson

Now
To each man's life there comes a time supreme,
One day, one night, one morning, or one noon,
One freighted hour, one moment opportune,
One space when fate goes tiding with the stream.
Happy the man who, knowing how to wait,
Knows also how to watch, and work, and stand
On life's broad deck alert, and on the prow
To seize the passing moment big with fate
From opportunity's extended hand
When the great clock of destiny strikes
  "Now."
Anonymous

Seize this very minute! What you can do,
or think you can do, begin it!
Wolfgang von Goethe

Courage

Courage isn't a brilliant dash,
A daring deed in a moment's flash;
It isn't an instantaneous thing
Born of despair with a sudden spring;
It isn't a creature of flickered hope
Or the final tug at a slipping rope;
But it's something deep in the soul of man
That is working always to serve some plan.

Courage isn't the last resort
In the work of life or the game of sport;
It isn't a thing that a man can call
At some future time when he's apt to fall;
If he hasn't it now, he will have it not
When the strain is great and the pace is hot.
For who would strive for a distant goal
Must always have courage within his soul.

Courage isn't a dazzling light
That flashes and passes away from sight;
It's a slow, unwavering, ingrained trait
With the patience to work and the strength
   to wait.
It's part of a man when his skies are blue;
It's part of him when he has work to do.
The brave man never is freed of it.
He has it when there is no need of it.

Courage was never designed for show;
It isn't a thing that can come and go;
It's written in victory and defeat
And every trial a man may meet.
It's part of his hours, his days and his years,
Back of his smiles and behind his tears.
Courage is more than a daring deed:
It's the breath of life and a strong
   man's creed.
      Edgar A. Guest

Life is an arrow--therefore you must know
What mark to aim at, how to use the bow,
Then draw it to the head and let it go.
      Henry van Dyke

The most precious things of life are near at hand. Each of you has the whole wealth of the Universe at your very door. All may be yours by stretching forth your hand and taking it.
      John Burroughs

Begin the Day With God

Every morning lean thine arms awhile
Upon the windowsill of heaven
And gaze upon thy Lord,
Then, with the vision in thy heart,
Turn strong to meet thy day.
      Thomas Blake

The things courage can do!

SIR JAMES M. BARRIE

Man's Heritage of Courage

There is, hidden deep within each one of us, a secret self which is ultimately invincible. No matter how heavy our burdens, how perplexing our problems, how intense the strain circumstance throws upon us, that inner self never wholly gives way. Time and again we catch glimpses of it--calm, poised, unafraid. It looks out at us from some secret window of the soul, like a strange, brave face gazing from the casement of an unexplored castle. Do you know the origin of this invincible inner self? For millions of years it has been slowly taking shape. Our far-off ancestors were primitive men who faced a desperately hard life. They lived in caves, in forests, and in wild hiding places among the hills. Day after day they had to fight for their very lives--now contending against animals, now against hostile fellow-men, now against the furious and as yet untamed forces of Nature. In that grim and never-ending struggle the individuals who lacked either the will to struggle or the ability to conquer were speedily and inevitably annihilated. Only those men and women who possessed the priceless qualities of strength, resourcefulness, and unwavering courage survived. From this selected group the next generation sprang, inheriting these peculiar and immensely valuable spiritual characteristics. Thus through a blind process of selective survival human beings gained, bit by bit, the phenomenal capacities for resistance, for struggle, and for conquest which they reveal today. It was the life-process itself, working for millions of years, that created the invincible inner self buried deep in the heart of each one of us.

James Gordon Gilkey

Give us, O Lord, steadfast hearts which no unworthy thought can drag downwards; unconquered hearts which no tribulation can wear out, upright hearts which no unworthy purpose may tempt aside. Bestow upon us also, O Lord our God, understanding to know Thee, diligence to seek Thee, wisdom to find Thee, and a faithfulness that may finally embrace Thee.

Thomas Aquinas

Truth

Truth is beautiful.
Ralph Waldo Emerson

TRUTH

Bear through sorrow, wrong and ruth,
In thy heart the dew of youth,
On thy lips the smile of truth.
Henry Wadsworth Longfellow

And God hath spread the earth as a carpet for you, that ye may walk therein through spacious paths.
from the Koran

An inexhaustible good nature is one of the most precious gifts of heaven, spreading itself like oil over the troubled sea of thought, and keeping the mind smooth and equable in the roughest weather.
Washington Irving

A loving heart is the truest wisdom.
Charles Dickens

The journey of a thousand miles begins with one step.
Lao-Tse

Truth

Vast is the sea—
Vast is the sky—
Vast is the roar—
Greater yet the sigh.

LEILANI TYSON PARKER

TRUTH

Truth, which only doth judge itself, teacheth, that the inquiry of Truth, which is the lovemaking, or wooing of it; the knowledge of Truth, which is the presence of it; and the belief of Truth, which is the enjoying of it; is the sovereign good of human nature. The first creature of God, in the works of the days, was the light of the sense; the last, was the light of reason; and His Sabbath work, ever since, is the illumination of His spirit. First He breathed light, upon the face, of the matter or chaos; then He breathed light, into the face of man; and still He breatheth and inspireth light, into the face of His chosen. The poet, that beautified the sect, that was otherwise inferior to the rest, saith yet excellently well: *It is a pleasure to stand upon the shore, and to see ships tost upon the sea: a pleasure to stand in the window of a castle, and to see a battle, and the adventures thereof, below: but no pleasure is comparable, to the standing, upon the vantage ground of Truth:* (a hill not to be commanded, and where the air is always clear, and serene;) *and to see the errors, and wanderings, and mists, and tempests, in the vale below:* so always, that this prospect, be with pity, and not with swelling, or pride. Certainly, it is Heaven upon earth, to have a man's mind move in charity, rest in providence, and turn upon the poles of Truth.

Francis Bacon

TRUTH

The most natural beauty in the world is honesty and moral truth; for all beauty is truth. True features make the beauty of a face; and true proportions the beauty of architecture; as true measures that of harmony and music. In poetry, which is all fable, truth still is the perfection.
Anthony A. Cooper

The knowledge of my own position and my own relations to the world, is truth. Thus every one may have his own truth, and yet it is the same truth.
Wolfgang von Goethe

What lies behind us and what lies before us are tiny matters compared to what lies within us.
William Morrow

Almost any man may like the spider spin from his own inwards his own citadel.
John Keats

Truth is the highest summit of art and of life.
Henri Frederic Amiel

We live in deeds, not in years; in thoughts, not breaths;
In feelings, not in figures on a dial.
We should count time by heart-throbs.
He most lives
Who thinks most, feels the noblest, acts the best.
Philip James Bailey

Brotherhood

The whole world and every human being in it is everybody's business.
William Saroyan

Needed: Good Samaritans
Open your eyes and look for some man, or some work for the sake of men, which needs a little time, a little friendship, a little sympathy, a little sociability, a little human toil. Perhaps it is a lonely person, or an embittered person, or an invalid, or some unfortunate inefficient, to whom you can be something. It may be an old man or it may be a child. Or some good work is in want of volunteers who will devote a free evening to it or will run on errands for it. Who can reckon up all the ways in which that priceless fund of impulse, man, is capable of exploitation! He is needed in every nook and corner. Therefore search and see if there is not some place where you may invest your humanity. Do not be put off if you find that you have to wait and to experiment. Be sure that you will have disappointments to endure. But do not be satisfied without some side line in which you may give yourself out as a man to men. There is one waiting for you if only you are willing to take it up in the right spirit.
Albert Schweitzer

I do not wish to treat friendships daintily, but with ruthless courage. Where they are real, they are not glass threads or frostwork, but the solidest things we know…. The sweet sincerity of joy and peace, which I draw from this alliance with my brother's soul, is the nut itself whereof all nature and all thought is but husk and shell. Happy is the house that shelters a friend!
Ralph Waldo Emerson

Lord, may I be wakeful at sunrise to begin a new day for thee; cheerful at sunset for having done my work for thee; thankful at moonrise and under starshine for the beauty of thy universe. And may I add what little may be in me to add to thy great world.
Abbot of Greve

If you approach each new person you meet in a spirit of adventure, you will find yourself endlessly fascinated by the new channels of thought and experience and personality that you encounter.
Eleanor Roosevelt

BROTHERHOOD

World Harmony

Our world is like an instrument
Whereon we each may play
The composition of a life
In measures grave and gay.

Our hearts conceive the melodies--
Our minds the motifs hold:
From white keys and from black keys
The music must unfold.

With human rights as pattern
For peace in every land--
In mounting unity and strength
The music shall expand.

A rhapsody of Brotherhood
Shall sound along the years--
And harmony on earth transcend
The music of the spheres.

Mamie Folsom Wynne

To smooth the rough and thorny way
   Where other feet begin to tread;
To feed some hungry soul each day
   With sympathy's sustaining bread.

Louisa May Alcott

Coming together is a beginning;
keeping together is progress;
working together is success.

HENRY FORD

If God is thy father, man is thy brother.
Alphonse de Lamartine

...thou shalt love thy neighbor as thyself.
Leviticus 19:18

What do we live for, if it is not to make life less difficult to each other.
George Eliot

The greatest satisfaction we can get out of life comes from building bridges - making the pathway of those who follow a little less bumpy.
William Feather

Look up and not down,
Look forward and not back,
Look out and not in,
Lend a hand.
Edward Everett Hale

The House by the Side of the Road

There are hermit souls that live withdrawn
In the place of their self-content;
There are souls like stars, that dwell apart,
In a fellowless firmament;
There are pioneer souls that blaze their paths
Where highways never ran--
But let me live by the side of the road
And be a friend to man.

Let me live in a house by the side of the road,
Where the race of men go by--
The men who are good and the men who are bad,
As good and as bad as I.
I would not sit in the scorner's seat,
Or hurl the cynic's ban--
Let me live in a house by the side of the road
And be a friend to man.

I see from my house by the side of the road,
By the side of the highway of life,
The men who press with the ardor of hope,
The men who are faint with the strife.
But I turn not away from their smiles nor their tears,
Both parts of an infinite plan--
Let me live in a house by the side of the road
And be a friend to man.

I know there are brook-gladdened meadows ahead,
And mountains of wearisome height;
That the road passes on through the long afternoon
And stretches away to the night.
But still I rejoice when the travelers rejoice,
And weep with the strangers that moan,
Nor live in my house by the side of the road
Like a man who dwells alone.

Let me live in my house by the side of the road,
Where the race of men go by--
They are good, they are bad, they are weak, they are strong,
Wise, foolish--so am I;
Then why should I sit in the scorner's seat,
Or hurl the cynic's ban?
Let me live in my house by the side of the road
And be a friend to man.

Sam Walter Foss

Belief

Walk on a rainbow trail, walk on a trail of song, and all about you will be beauty. There is a way out of every dark mist, over a rainbow trail.

Navajo Song

Write it on your heart that every day is the best day of the year.
Ralph Waldo Emerson

Live every day of your life as though you expected to live forever.
Douglas MacArthur

Come with us to the field, or go with our brothers to the sea and cast your net. For the land and the sea shall be bountiful to you even as to us.
Kahlil Gibran

Light Shining Out of Darkness
God moves in a mysterious way
    His wonders to perform;
He plants His footsteps in the sea
    And rides upon the storm.

Deep in the unfathomable mines
    Of never-failing skill
He treasures up His bright designs
    And works His sovereign will.

Blind unbelief is sure to err
    And scan His work in vain;
God is His own interpreter,
    And He will make it plain.
William Cowper

My Creed
To live as gently as I can;
To be, no matter where, a man;
To take what comes of good or ill
And cling to faith and honor still;
To do my best, and let that stand
The record of my brain and hand;
And then, should failure come to me,
Still work and hope for victory.

To have no secret place wherein
I stoop unseen to shame or sin;
To be the same when I'm alone
As when my every deed is known;
To live undaunted, unafraid
Of any step that I have made;
To be without pretense or sham
Exactly what men think I am.

To leave some simple mark behind
To keep my having lived in mind;
If enmity to aught I show,
To be an honest, generous foe,
To play my little part, nor whine
That greater honors are not mine.
This, I believe, is all I need
For my philosophy and creed.
Edgar A. Guest

> *Man is what he believes.*
>
> ANTON CHEKHOV

Blessed be the name of God for ever and ever, to whom belong wisdom and might. To thee, O God of my fathers, I give thanks and praise, for thou hast given me wisdom and strength.
Daniel 2:20,23

We are members of one great body, planted by nature in a mutual love and fitted for a social life. We must consider that we were born for the good of the whole.
Seneca

Of Belief
Every one trusts to somewhat. As for honour and esteem and popularity, they are airy, vain things; but riches seem a more solid work and fence, yet they are but a tower in conceit, not really: "The rich man's wealth is his strong city, and as a high wall in his own conceit; but the name of the Lord is a strong tower indeed." This is the thing that all seek, some fence and fixing; and here it is. We call you not to vexation and turmoil, but *from* it, and, as St. Paul said, "Whom ye ignorantly worship, Him declare I unto you." Ye blindly and fruitlessly seek after the show and shadow instead of the substance. The true aiming at this fixedness of mind will secure that, though they that aim fall short, yet by the way they will light on very pretty things that have some virtue in them; as they that seek the philosopher's stone. But the believer hath the thing, the secret itself of tranquility and joy, and this turns all into gold, even iron chains into a crown of gold. "While we look not at the things which are seen, but at the things which are not seen."

This is the blessed and safe estate of believers. Who can think they have a sad, heavy life? Oh! it is the only lightsome, sweet, cheerful condition in the world! The rest of men are poor, rolling, unstayed things, every report shaking them "as the leaves of trees are shaken with the wind," yea, lighter than these, they are as the "chaff that the wind drives to and fro" at its pleasure. Would men but reflect and look in upon their own hearts, it is a wonder what vain childish things the most would find there, glad and sorry at things as light as the toys of children, at which they laugh and cry in a breath. How easily is the heart puffed up with a thing or word that pleaseth us, bladder-like, swelled with a little air, and it shrinks in again in discouragement and fear upon the touch of a needle point, which gives that air some vent.
Robert Leighton

A Summer Creed
I believe in the flowers, and their glorious indifference to the changes of the morrow.

I believe in the birds, and their implicit trust in the loving Providence that feeds them.

I believe in the prayer-chanting brooks, as they murmur a sweet hope of finding the far distant sea to which they patiently run.

I believe in the whispering winds, for they teach me to listen to the still small voice within my feverish soul.

I believe in the vagrant clouds, as they remind me that life, like a summer day, must have some darkness to reveal its hidden meaning.

I believe in the soft-speaking rains, accented with warm tears, telling me that nothing will grow save it be fertilized with tears.

I believe in the golden hush of the sunsets, reflecting a momentary glory of that world beyond my little horizon.

I believe in the soft-falling dew, revealing the infinite spring of living waters for things parched and withered.

I believe in the holiness of twilight, as it gives me a sense of the presence of God, and I know that I am not alone. And whatever else I believe is enshrined in those abiding feelings that lie too deep for words.

W. Waldemar W. Argow

Beauty

Nothing is more beautiful than the loveliness of the woods before sunrise.

George Washington Carver

Youth's Dream of Beauty

"My dear son, God has put wisdom in my head and beauty into yours. Wisdom is needed for the governance of this world, but beauty is needed for its existence. In arid deserts there is no life. Birds do not sing in the dark of night. Show me a waste country, and I'll show you a brutal people. No faith can live that is not beautiful....

"The beauty God has put in your heart, child, you must always keep...I will not keep you any longer. Only to say this, and this is the chiefest thing: never let your dream be taken from you. Keep it unspotted from the world. In darkness and in tribulation it will go with you as a friend; but in wealth and power hold fast to it, for then is danger. Let not the mists of the world, the gay diversions, the little trifles, draw you from glory.

"Remember!"

Donn Byrne

RALPH WALDO EMERSON

If eyes were made for seeing, then Beauty is its own excuse for being.

Beauty

I was visited, as I sat in my room today, by one of those sudden impressions of rare beauty that come and go like flashes, and which leave one desiring a similar experience. The materials of the impression were simple and familiar enough. My room looks out into a little court; there is a plot of grass, and to the right of it an old stone-built wall, close against which stands a row of aged lime-trees. Straight opposite, at right angles to the wall, is the east side of the Hall, with its big plain traceried window enlivened with a few heraldic shields of stained glass. While I was looking out today there came a flying burst of sun, and the little corner became a sudden feast of delicate colour; the rich green of the grass, the foliage of the lime-trees, their brown wrinkled stems, the pale moss on the walls, the bright points of colour in the emblazonries of the window, made a sudden delicate harmony of tints. I had seen the place a hundred times before without ever guessing what a perfect picture it made.

What a strange power the perception of beauty is! It seems to ebb and flow like some secret tide, independent alike of health or disease, of joy or sorrow. There are times in our lives when we seem to go singing on our way, and when the beauty of the world sets itself like a quiet harmony to the song we uplift.

A. C. Benson

Beauty
There is beauty in homely things
which many people have never seen:
> Sunlight through a jar of beach-plum jelly;
> A rainbow in soapsuds in dishwater;
> An egg yolk in a blue bowl;
> White ruffled curtains sifting moonlight;
> The color of cranberry glass;
> A little cottage with blue shutters;
> Crimson roses in an old stone crock;
> The smell of newly baked bread;
> Candlelight on old brass;
> The soft brown of a cocker's eyes.
>> *Peter Marshall*

The Divine beauty is not adorned with any shape or endowment of form, or with any beauty of color, but is contemplated as excellence in unspeakable bliss.
> *Saint Gregory of Nyssa*

The beautiful is a phenomenon which is never apparent of itself, but is reflected in a thousand different works of the creator.
> *Wolfgang von Goethe*

To Helen
Helen, thy beauty is to me
> Like those Nicéan barks of yore,
That gently, o'er a perfumed sea,
> The weary, way-worn wanderer bore
> To his own native shore.

On desperate seas long wont to roam,
> Thy hyacinth hair, thy classic face,
Thy Naiad airs have brought me home
> To the glory that was Greece,
> And the grandeur that was Rome.

Lo! in yon brilliant window-niche
> How statue-like I see thee stand,
The agate lamp within thy hand!
> Ah, Psyche, from the regions which
> Are Holy-Land!
>> *Edgar Allan Poe*

Beauty is undoubtedly the signature of the Master to the work in which he has put his soul; it is the divine spirit manifested.
> *Honoré de Balzac*

She Walks in Beauty
She walks in beauty like the night
Of cloudless climes and starry skies;
And all that's best of dark and bright
Meet in her aspect and her eyes:
Thus mellowed to that tender light
Which heaven to gaudy day denies.
> *Lord Byron*

Beauty

Beauty is an all-pervading presence. It unfolds to the numberless flowers of the Spring; it waves in the branches of the trees and in the green blades of grass; it haunts the depths of the earth and the sea, and gleams out in the hues of the shell and the precious stone. And not only these minute objects, but the ocean, the mountains, the clouds, the heavens, the stars, the rising and the setting sun all overflow with beauty. The universe is its temple; and those men who are alive to it can not lift their eyes without feeling themselves encompassed with it on every side. Now, this beauty is so precious, the enjoyment it gives so refined and pure, so congenial without tenderest and noblest feelings, and so akin to worship, that it is painful to think of the multitude of men as living in the midst of it, and living almost as blind to it as if, instead of this fair earth and glorious sky, they were tenants of a dungeon. An infinite joy is lost to the world by the want of culture of this spiritual endowment. The greatest truths are wronged if not linked with beauty, and they win their way most surely and deeply into the soul when arrayed in this their natural and fit attire.

William Ellery Channing

Beauty is eternity gazing at itself in a mirror.

KAHLIL GIBRAN

We are living in a world of beauty but how few of us open our eyes to see it! What a different place this would be if our senses were trained to see and hear! We are the heirs of wonderful treasures from the past: treasures of literature and of the arts. They are ours for the asking--all our own to have and to enjoy, if only we desire them enough.

Lorado Taft

Beautiful Things

Beautiful faces are those that wear--
It matters little if dark or fair--
Whole-souled honesty printed there.

Beautiful eyes are those that show,
Like crystal panes where hearthfires glow,
Beautiful thoughts that burn below.

Beautiful lips are those whose words
Leap from the heart like songs of birds,
Yet whose utterance prudence girds.

Beautiful hands are those that do
Work that is honest and brave and true,
Moment by moment the long day through.

Beautiful feet are those that go
On kindly ministries to and fro,
Down lowliest ways, if God wills it so.

Beautiful shoulders are those that bear
Ceaseless burdens of homely care
With patient grace and daily prayer.

Beautiful lives are those that bless
Silent rivers of happiness,
Whose hidden fountains but few may guess.

Beautiful twilight at set of sun,
Beautiful goal with race well won,
Beautiful rest with work well done.

Beautiful graves where grasses creep,
Where brown leaves fall, where drifts lie deep
Over worn-out hands--oh! beautiful sleep!

Ellen P. Allerton

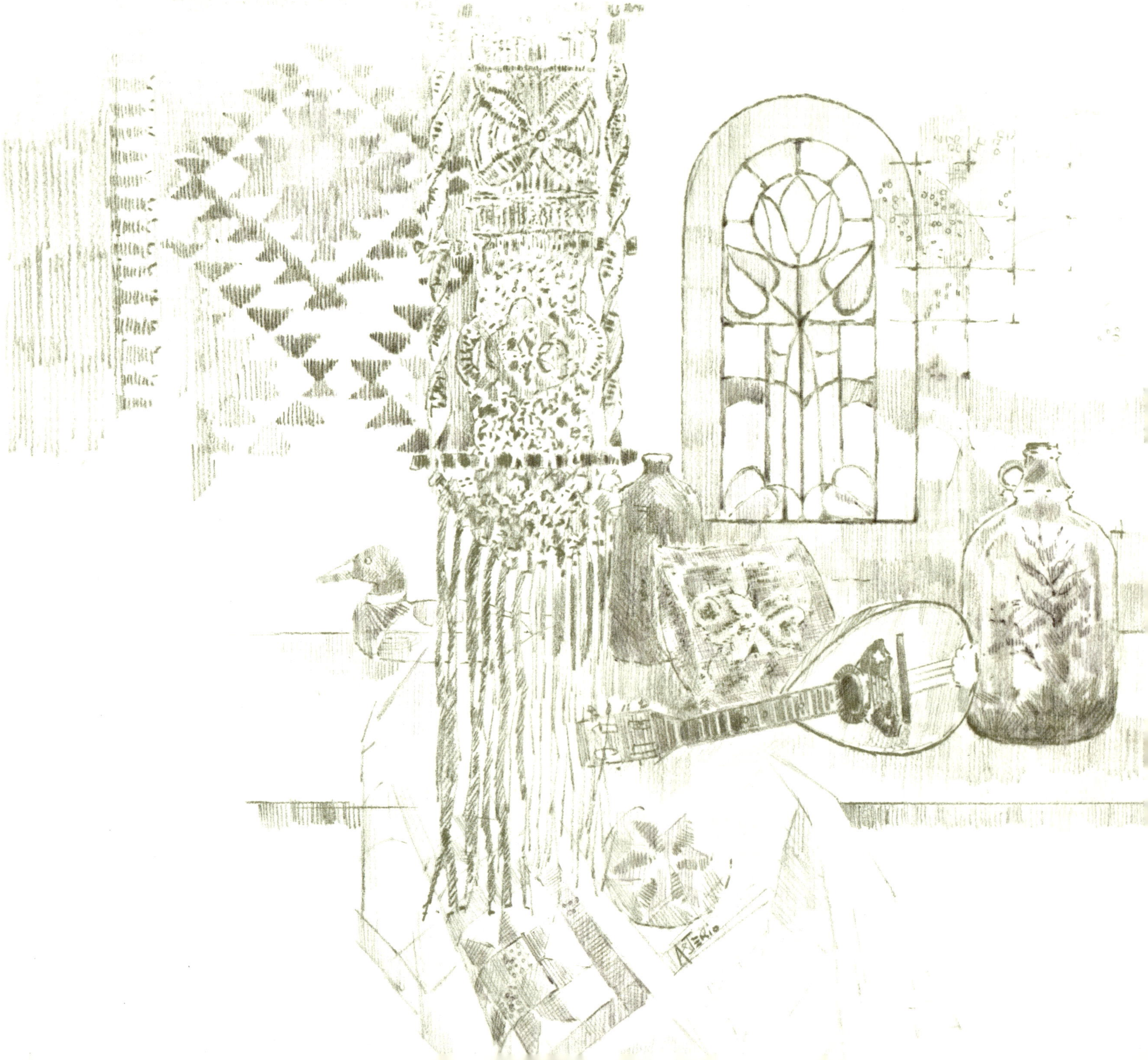

Art

The pleasure of creating beautiful things…
the greatest pleasure in the world.
William Morris

ART

Art does not reproduce the visible; rather, it makes visible.
Paul Klee

Art is man added to nature.
Francis Bacon

When tillage begins, other arts follow. The farmers, therefore, are the founders of civilization.
Daniel Webster

A man's work whether in music, painting, or literature, is always a portrait of himself.
Samuel Butler

But words are things;
    And a small drop of ink,
Falling like dew upon a thought, produces
That which makes thousands,
    Perhaps millions, think.
Lord Byron

We will be happy if we can get around to the idea that art is not an outside and extra thing; that it is a natural outcome of a state of being; that the state of being is the important thing; that a man can be a carpenter and be a great.
Robert Henri

All the arts are brothers; each one is a light to the others.
Voltaire

Art is in love with luck, and luck with art.
Agathon

New artists must break a hole in the subconscious and go fishing there.
Robert Beverly Hale

A photograph is a portrait painted by the sun.
André Dupin

To draw, you must close your eyes and sing.
PABLO PICASSO

The books that charmed us in youth recall the delight ever afterwards; we are hardly persuaded there are any like them, any deserving equally our affections. Fortunate if the best fall in our way during this susceptible and forming period of our lives.
Amos Bronson Alcott

Remember Me

I am Music--oldest of the arts. When all was void--the Morning Stars sang together at the creation of the world!

I am Music--for all who listen. I am part of every human experience from the cradle--on to the grave.

I am Music--the tender lullaby the mother croons to her cradled babe, lulling it to restful slumber and to rosy dreams.

I am Music--ringing the merry bells of youth--as our young go faring forth so gallantly along the paths of destiny.

I am Music--the harmonious avowal of love which binds two pulsing hearts together in a union deathless and inseparable.

I am Music--sounding the tocsin call to warriors. With martial beat, I send them marching on to battle and to victory. I chant my solemn requiem over the graves of the heroic dead.

I am Music--giving consolation to the bereaved and sorrowful. I cheer the long hours of loneliness and pain--bringing my interludes of quietness and calm to the aged and the oppressed.

I am Music--proclaiming the steadfast faith of believing hearts. I celebrate the beauty of Christian ordinances. I reveal the unalterable truth--that enables the humblest clod to become regenerate, and to behold the wonders of a living God!

I am Music--I was from the beginning and shall be to the end of man's existence. Happy are they whose lives are attuned to my cadences. For them there opens a shining way--a lyrical rainbow--spanning earth and heaven with majesty, joyousness and Peace, Amen.

Mamie Folsom Wynne

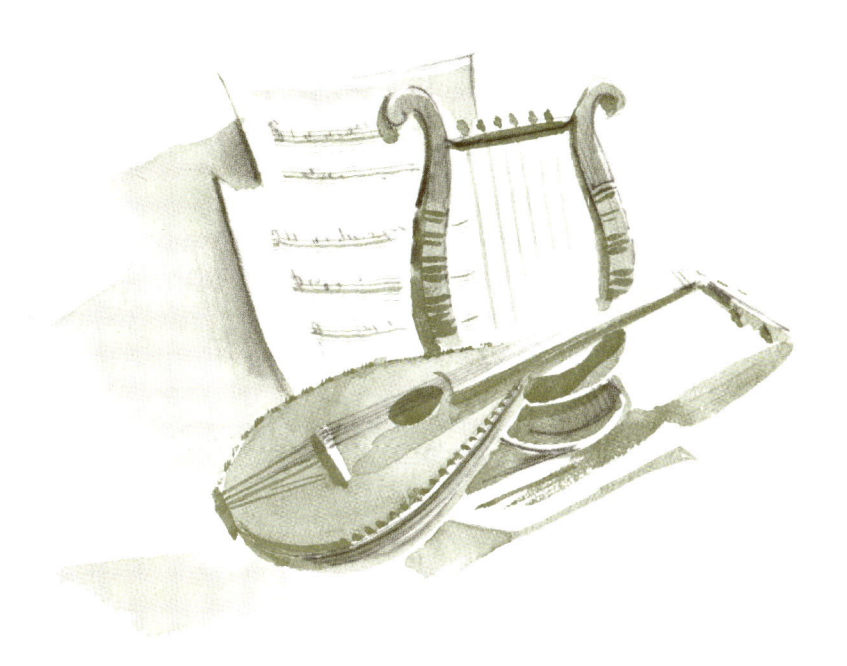

Literature's Service

The chief trait of any given poet is always the spirit he brings to the observation of Humanity and Nature--the mood out of which he contemplates his subjects. What kind of temper and what amount of faith report these things? Up to how recent a date is the song carried? What the equipment, and special raciness of the singer--what his tinge of coloring? The last value of artistic expressers, past and present--Greek aesthetes, Shakespeare--or in our own day Tennyson, Victor Hugo, Carlyle, Emerson--is certainly involv'd in such questions. I say the profoundest service that poems or any other writings can do for their reader is not merely to satisfy the intellect, or supply something polish'd or interesting, nor even to depict great passions, or persons or events, but to fill him with vigorous and clean manliness, religiousness, and give him *good heart* as a radical possession and habit. The educated world seems to have been growing more and more ennuied for ages, leaving to our time the inheritance of it all. Fortunately there is the original inexhaustible fund of buoyancy, normally resident in the race, forever eligible to be appeal'd to and relied on.

Walt Whitman

The Poet

The poet is chiefly distinguished from other men by a greater promptness to think and feel without immediate external excitement, and a greater power in expressing such thoughts and feelings as are produced in him in that manner. But these passions and thoughts and feelings are the general passions and thoughts and feelings of men. And with what are they connected? Undoubtedly with our moral sentiments and animal sensations, and with the causes which excite these; with the operations of the elements, and the appearances of the visible universe; with storm and sunshine, with the revolutions of the seasons, with cold and heat, with loss of friends and kindred, with injuries and resentments, gratitude and hope, with fear and sorrow. These, and the like, are the sensations and objects which the poet describes, as they are the sensations of other men and the objects which interest them.

William Wordsworth

God

The Lord has turned all our sunsets into sunrises.

Clement of Alexandria

Because There Is a God

Now he had learnt to see the great, the eternal, and the infinite in everything; and naturally, therefore, in order to see it, to revel in its contemplation, he flung aside the telescope through which he had hitherto been gazing over men's heads and looked joyfully at the ever changing, ever grand, unfathomable, and infinite life around him. And the closer he looked at it, the calmer and happier he was. The terrible question that had shattered all his intellectual edifices in old days, the question: What for? had no existence for him now. To that question, What for? he had now always ready in his soul the simple answer: Because there is a God, that God without whom not one hair of a man's head falls.

Leo Tolstoy

God
Conceived the world,
That was poetry;
He formed it,
That was sculpture;
He colored it,
That was painting;
He peopled it with living beings,
That was the grand, divine, Eternal drama.

CHARLOTTE CUSHMAN

God's Will

What we see here of this world is but an expression of God's will, so to speak--a beautiful earth and sky and sea--beautiful affections and sorrows, wonderful changes and developments of creation, suns rising, stars shining, birds singing, clouds and shadows changing and fading, people loving each other, smiling and crying, the multiplied phenomena of Nature, multiplied in fact and in fancy, in Art and Science, in every way that a man's intellect or education can be brought to bear. And who is to say that we are to ignore all this, or not value them and love them, because there is another unknown world yet to come? Why, that unknown future world is but a manifestation of God Almighty's will, and a development of Nature, neither more nor less than this in which we are, and an angel glorified or a sparrow on a gutter are equally part of His creation. The light upon all the saints in Heaven is just as much and no more God's work, and the sun which shall shine tomorrow upon this infinitesimal speck of creation.

William Makepeace Thackeray

God sent His singers upon earth
With songs of sadness and of mirth,
That they might touch the hearts of men
And bring them back to heaven again.
         Henry Wadsworth Longfellow

The first of all beautiful things is the continual possession of God.
         Saint Gregory Nazianzen

An old mystic says somewhere, "God is an unutterable sigh in the innermost depths of the soul." With still greater justice, we may reverse the proposition and say the soul is a never ending sigh after God.
         Theodore Christlieb

In the faces of men and women I see God.
         WALT WHITMAN

Could we with ink the ocean fill
  Were every blade of grass a quill
  Were the world of parchment made
  And every man a scribe by trade
To write the love of God above
  Would drain the ocean dry;
  Nor would the scroll contain the whole
  Though stretched from sky to sky.
         Meir Ben Isaac Neherai

Wait On
To talk with God,
No breath is lost--
   Talk on!
To walk with God,
No strength is lost--
   Walk on!
To wait on God,
No time is lost--
   Wait on!
from the Hindi

God's in His Heaven
And all's right with the World.
Robert Browning

God is a circle whose center is everywhere
and its circumference nowhere.
Empedocles

My concern is not whether God is on our side; my great concern is to be on God's side, for God is always right.
Abraham Lincoln

God helps those who help themselves.
It is not necessary to light a candle in the sun.
Algernon Sidney

The mountains are God's thoughts piled up.
The ocean is God's thoughts spread out.
The flowers are God's thoughts in bloom.
The dewdrops are God's thoughts in pearls.
Samuel Jones

God--That unity of bests.
Elizabeth Barrett Browning

God is within us: He is that inner presence which makes us admire the beautiful, which rejoices us when we have done right and consoles us for not sharing the happiness of the wicked.
Eugène Delacroix

Hope

Hope is the dream of a man awake.
Matthew Prior

HOPE

True hope is swift and flies with swallows'
wings; kings it makes gods, and meaner
creatures kings.
William Shakespeare

Hope is the thing with feathers
That perches in the soul,
And sings the tune without the words,
And never stops at all,

And sweetest in the gale is heard;
And sore must be the storm
That could abash the little bird
That kept so many warm.

I've heard it in the chillest land,
And on the strangest sea;
Yet, never, in extremity,
It asked a crumb of me.
Emily Dickinson

The word which God has written on the
brow of every man is Hope.
Victor Hugo

Hope, like a gleaming taper's light,
   Adorns and cheers our way;
And still, as darker grows the night,
   Emits a brighter ray.
Oliver Goldsmith

Hope is like the sun, which, as we journey
toward it, casts the shadow of our burden
behind us.
Samuel Smiles

Credo
I cannot find my way: there is no star
In all the shrouded heavens anywhere;
And there is not a whisper in the air
Of any living voice but one so far
That I can hear it only as a bar
Of lost, imperial music, played when fair
And angel fingers wove, and unaware,
Dead leaves to garlands where no roses are.

No, there is not a glimmer, nor a call,
For one that welcomes, welcomes when he fears,
The black and awful chaos of the night;
But through it all,--above, beyond it all--
I know the far-sent message of the years,
I feel the coming glory of the Light!
Edwin Arlington Robinson

I Hope
I hope that I shall never tire
Of watching colors in the fire.
I hope I shall not be too old
To see the lilac-stars unfold,
Or find the pear tree wearing white
When spring is summer overnight.
When I am tired of rapture,
Let me die then.
Let me never see the frost
Or a fern again.
When songs do not delight,
When waves that lip the pier,
Or driftwood fires,
Or faces
Are no longer dear--
Let me die quickly;
Let me not know
The eyes of friends,
Candlelight, silence, or snow.
Mildred Bowers Armstrong

HOPE!--Who is insensible to the music of that word? What bosom has not kindled under its utterance? Poetry has sung of it; music has warbled it; oratory has lavished on it its bewitching strains. Fled from the world, Hope, with her elastic dreams, said that when all other divinities fled from the world, Hope, with her elastic step and radiant countenance and lustrous attire, lingered behind. Hope! well may we personify thee, lighting up thy altar-fires in this dark world, and dropping a live coal into many desolate hearts; gladdening the sick chamber with visions of returning health; illuminating with rays, brighter than the sunbeam, the captive's cell; crowding the broken slumbers of the soldier by his bivouac-fire with pictures of his sunny home and his own joyous return. Hope! drying the tear on the cheek of woe! As the black clouds of sorrow break and fall to the earth, arching the descending drops with thine own beauteous rainbow! Ay, more, standing with thy lamp in thy hand by the gloomy realms of Hades, kindling thy torch at Nature's funeral pile, and opening vistas through the gates of glory! If Hope, even with reference to present and infinite things, be an emotion so joyous--if uninspired poetry can sing so sweetly of its delights, what must be the believer's hope, the hope which has God for its object and Heaven its consummation?
John MacDuff

Hope is the better half of courage. Hope! has it not sustained the work and given the fainting heart time and patience to outwit the chances and changes of life.
Honoré de Balzac

Eternity is the divine treasure house, and hope is the window, by means of which mortals are permitted to see, as through a glass darkly, the things which God is preparing.
Mountford

Far away there in the sunshine are my highest aspirations. I may not reach them, but I can look up and see their beauty, believe in them, and try to follow where they lead.
Louisa May Alcott

Lord, grant that I may always desire more than I can accomplish.
MICHELANGELO

Expectancy

The life in us is like the water in the river. It may rise this year higher than man has ever known it and flood the parched uplands; even this may be the eventful year, which will drown out all our muskrats. It was not always dry land where we dwell. I see far inland the banks which the stream anciently washed, before science began to record its freshets. Every one has heard the story which has gone the rounds of New England, of a strong and beautiful bug which came out of the dry leaf of an old table of apple-tree wood, which had stood in a farmer's kitchen for sixty years, first in Connecticut, and afterward in Massachusetts--from an egg deposited in the living tree many years earlier still, as appeared by counting the annual layers beyond it; which was heard gnawing out for several weeks, hatched perchance by the heat of an urn. Who does not feel his faith in a resurrection and immortality strengthened by hearing of this? Who knows what beautiful and winged life, whose egg has been buried for ages under many concentric layers of woodenness in the dead dry life of society, deposited at first in the alburnum of the green and living tree, which has been gradually converted into the semblance of its well-seasoned tomb--heard perchance gnawing out now for years by the astonished family of man, as they sat round the festive board--may unexpectedly come forth from amidst society's most trivial and handselled furniture, to enjoy its perfect summer life at last!

I do not say that John or Jonathan will realize this; but such is the character of that morrow which mere lapse of time can never make to dawn. The light which puts out our eyes is darkness to us. Only that day dawns to which we are awake. There is more day to dawn. The sun is but a morning star.

Henry David Thoreau

The Art of Hope

The well-known maxim, "While there is life there is hope," has deeper meaning in reverse: "While there is hope there is life."

Hope comes first, life follows. Hope gives power to life. Hope rouses life to continue, to expand, to grow, to reach out, to go on.

Hope sees a light where there isn't any.

Hope lights candles in millions of despairing hearts.

Hope is the miracle medicine of the mind. It inspires the will to live. Hope is the physician's strongest ally.

Hope is man's shield and buckler against defeat.

"Hope," wrote Alexander Pope, "springs eternal in the human breast." And as long as it does man will triumph and move forward.

Hope never sounds retreat. Hope keeps the banners flying.

Hope revives ideals, renews dreams, revitalizes visions.

Hope scales the peak, wrestles with the impossible, achieves the highest aim.

"The word which God has written on the brow of every man," wrote Victor Hugo, "is Hope." As long as man has hope no situation is hopeless.

Wilferd A. Peterson

Home

<big>H</big>ome is where the heart is.
Pliny

HOME

Home, Sweet Home

'Mid pleasures and palaces though we may roam,
Be it ever so humble, there's no place like home;
A charm from the sky seems to hallow us there,
Which, seek through the world, is ne'er met with elsewhere.
    Home, home, sweet, sweet home!
There's no place like home, oh, there's no place like home!

An exile from home, splendor dazzles in vain;
Oh, give me my lowly thatched cottage again!
The birds singing gayly, that came at my call--
Give me them--and the peace of mind, dearer than all!
    Home, home, sweet, sweet home!
There's no place like home, oh, there's no place like home!

I gaze on the moon as I tread the drear wild,
And feel that my mother now thinks of her child,
As she looks on that moon from our own cottage door
Thro' the woodbine, whose fragrance shall cheer me no more.
    Home, home, sweet, sweet home!
There's no place like home, oh, there's no place like home!

How sweet 'tis to sit 'neath a fond father's smile,
And the caress of a mother to soothe and beguile!
Let others delight 'mid new pleasure to roam,
But give me, oh, give me, the pleasures of home,
    Home, home, sweet, sweet home!
There's no place like home, oh, there's no place like home!

To thee I'll return, overburdened with care;
The heart's dearest solace will smile on me there;
No more from that cottage again will I roam;
Be it ever so humble, there's no place like home.
    Home, home, sweet, sweet home!
There's no place like home, oh, there's no place like home!

John Howard Payne

Care-Free Youth

The skies are blue and the sun is out and the
　grass is green and soft
And the old charm's back in the apple tree and it
　calls a boy aloft;
And the same low voice that the old don't hear,
　but the care-free youngsters do,
Is calling them to the fields and streams and the
　joys that once I knew.
And if youth be wild desire for play and care is
　the mark of men,
Beneath the skin that Time has tanned I'm a madcap
　youngster then.

Far richer than king with his crown of gold and
　his heavy weight of care
Is the sunburned boy with his stone-bruised feet
　and his tousled shock of hair;
For the king can hear but the cry of hate or the
　sickly sound of praise,
And lost to him are the voices sweet that called
　in his boyhood days.
Far better than ruler, with pomp and power and
　riches, is it to be
The urchin gay in his tattered clothes that is
　climbing the apple tree.

Oh, once I heard all the calls that come to the
　quick, glad ears of boys,
And a certain spot on the river bank told me of
　its many joys,
And certain fields and certain trees were loyal
　friends to me,
And I knew the birds, and I owned a dog, and we
　both could hear and see.
Oh, never from tongues of men have dropped such
　messages wholly glad
As the things that live in the great outdoors once
　told to a little lad.

And I'm sorry for him who cannot hear what the
　tall trees have to say,
Who is deaf to the call of a running stream and
　the lanes that lead to play.
The boy that shins up the faithful elm or sprawls
　on a river bank
Is more richly blessed with the joys of life than
　any old man of rank.
For youth is the golden time of life, and this
　battered old heart of mine
Beats fast to the march of its old-time joys
　when the sun begins to shine.

Edgar A. Guest

Happy homes are built of blocks of patience.

HAROLD E. KOHN

The House Beautiful
The Crown of the house is Godliness.
The Beauty of the house is Order.
The Glory of the house is Hospitality.
The Blessing of the house is Contentment.
Old Inscription

But what on earth is half so dear--
So longed for--
As the hearth of home?
Emily Bronte

Every house where love abides and
friendship is a guest, is surely home, and
home, sweet home; for there the heart
can rest.
Henry van Dyke

Sweet is the smile of home;
   the mutual look
When hearts are of each other
   sure.
John Keble

The Blue Bowl
All day I did the little things,
The little things that do not show;
I brought the kindling for the fire,
I set the candles in a row,
I filled a bowl with marigolds--
The shallow bowl you love the best--
And made the house a pleasant place
Where weariness may take its rest.

The hours sped on, my eager feet
Could not keep pace with my desire.
So much to do, so little time!
I could not let my body tire;
Yet, when the coming of the night
Blotted the garden from my sight,
And on the narrow, graveled walks
Between the guarding flower stalks
I heard your step; I was not through
With services I meant for you.

You came into the quiet room
That glowed enchanted with the bloom
Of yellow flame. I saw your face,
Illumined by the firelit space,
Slowly grow still and comforted--
"It's good to be at home," you said.
Blanche Bane Kuder

Home, the spot of earth supremely blest--
a dearer, sweeter spot than all the rest.
Robert Montgomery

The dear things of home have eternal life.
Motto on a Sundial

Home

It takes a heap o' livin' in a house t' make it home,
A heap o' sun an' shadder, an' ye sometimes have t' roam
Afore ye really 'preciate the things ye lef' behind,
An' hunger fer 'em somehow, with 'em allus on yer mind.
It don't make any differunce how rich ye get t' be,
How much yer chairs an' tables cost, how great yer luxury;
It ain't home t' ye, though it be the palace of a king,
Until somehow yer soul is sort o' wrapped round everything.

Home ain't a place that gold can buy or get up in a minute;
Afore it's home there's got t' be a heap o' livin' in it;
Within the walls there's got t' be some babies born, and then
Right there ye've got t' bring 'em up t' women good, an' men;
And gradjerly, as time goes on, ye find ye wouldn't part
With anything they ever used--they've grown into yer heart:
The old high chairs, the playthings, too, the little shoes they wore
Ye hoard; an' if ye could ye'd keep the thumbmarks on the door.

Ye've got t' weep t' make it home, ye've got t' sit an' sigh
An' watch beside a loved one's bed, an' know that Death is nigh;
An' in the stillness o' the night t' see Death's angel come,
An' close the eyes o' her that smiled,
    an' leave her sweet voice dumb.
For these are scenes that grip the heart,
    an' when yer tears are dried,
Ye find the home is dearer than it was,
    an' sanctified;
An' tuggin' at ye always are the pleasant memories
O' her that was an' is no more--
    ye can't escape from these.

Ye've got to sing an' dance fer years,
    ye've got t' romp an' play,
An' learn t' love the things ye have by usin' 'em each day;
Even the roses round the porch must blossom year by year
Afore they 'come a part o' ye, suggestin' someone dear
Who used t' love 'em long ago, and trained 'em just t' run
The way they do, so's they would get the early mornin' sun;
Ye've got to love each brick an' stone from cellar up t' dome:
It takes a heap o' livin' in a house t' make it home.

Edgar A. Guest

There is no place more delightful than home.

CICERO

Home
This is the true nature of home--it is the place of Peace; the shelter, not only from all injury, but from all terror, doubt, and division. In so far as it is not this, it is not home: so far as the anxieties of the outer life penetrate into it, and the inconsistently minded, unknown, unloved, or hostile society of the outer world is allowed by either husband or wife to cross the threshold, it ceases to be home; it is then only a part of that outer world which you have roofed over and lighted fire in. But so far as it is a sacred place, a vestal temple, a temple of the hearth watched over by Household Gods, before whose faces none may come but those whom they can receive with love--so far as it is this, and roof and fire are types only of a nobler shade and light--shade as of the rock in a weary land, and light as of the Pharos in the stormy sea-- so far it vindicates the name, and fulfills the praise, of home.

And wherever a true wife comes, this home is always round her. The stars only may be over her head; the glowworm in the night-cold grass may be the only fire at her foot; but home is yet wherever she is; and for a noble woman it stretches far round her, better than ceiled with cedar, or painted with vermilion, shedding its quiet light far, for those whose else were homeless.
John Ruskin

You can no more measure a home by inches, or weigh it by ounces, than you can set up the boundaries of a summer breeze, or calculate the fragrance of a rose. Home is the love which is in it.
Edward Whiting

Home is the place where character is built, where sacrifices to contribute to the happiness of others are made, and where love has taken up its abode.
Elijah Kellogg

Seasons

New Day Dawning

What will be the morning's mood —
What will she wear today?
She might sit all alone and brood
In veils of misty gray.

She might awaken bright and bold,
Her dawning all ablaze
With robes of flaming pink and gold
As in her autumn days.

She might be lost in breathless hush,
A maiden sweet and shy
Who wears a tender rosy blush
That glows across the sky.

Or she might wrap herself in clouds
Of purple for a while,
Then cast aside her darkened shroud
And wear a golden smile.

Nell Reneau

Spring

Season of mists and mellow fruitfulness.
John Keats

Spring
Now fades the last long streak of snow,
    Now burgeons every maze of quick
    About the flowering squares, and thick
By ashen roots the violets blow.

Now rings the woodland loud and long,
    The distance takes a lovelier hue,
    And drowned in yonder living blue
The lark becomes a sightless song.

Now dance the lights on lawn and lea,
    The flocks are whiter down the vale,
    And milkier every milky sail,
On winding stream or distant sea;

Where now the seamew pipes, or dives
    In yonder greening gleam, and fly
    The happy birds, that change their sky
To build and brood, that live their lives.

From land to land; and in my breast
    Spring wakens too; and my regret
    Becomes an April violet,
And buds and blossoms like the rest.
Alfred Tennyson

Spring
In emerald shoes Spring pirouettes
Upon a crystal stage,
Then lifts enchanting hands to free
A singing scarlet page.

From barren stalks she draws bright flags
As sun spotlights her art,
And with a violet-scented kiss
She melts King Winter's heart.
Louise Hajek

When I was a kid, on a fresh Spring day
I useta go at sun-up to get the smell o' May;
And say! The waves o' perfumes that they would always be!
All the flowers in the world, so it looked to me,
Was mixed with the good ol' fresh-dug ground--
A kind of smell that God his self would like to have around.

I couldn't find the smell o' the Spring today.
Somethin' is happened--took it clean away.
The same kinda apple-blooms was shinin' on the tree--
I guess it ain't the Spring changed--it must be me.
Take my money--take my house--every single thing--
Oh, Mr. Yesterday!--Let me smell the Spring!
John V. A. Weaver

Summer

I can't understand about the Fall.
　　Why everythin's so wild and bright
　　　　and gay!
It's like the world was at a Fancy Ball,
　　And nothin' mattered excep' just to play.

The birds is singin' crazy bran'-new tunes;
　　The bushes got red ribbons for their hair;
The trees looks like they bought theirself
　　　　balloons,
　　Scarlet and yellow wavin' in the air.

They know they got old Winter fooled,
　　　　I s'pose.
　　　　And though he'll come some day and tear
　　　　　　and roar,
Bust up their party, ruin their pretty clo'es,
　　It'll be all right when Spring comes back
　　　　once more.

And still it makes me all choke up, to know
All lovely things that's now, has got to go.
　　　　　　　　　　John V. A. Weaver

Summer
Quickly, Summer, safely gather
Every cherished bit of beauty
From each shortened day;
Examine each with tenderness
Before it's put away.
Hold the magic of your mornings,
Guard your heaven's brilliant blue,
Lock the lazy haze of evening
Close against the warmth of you.
Pack each precious well-loved moment,
Sprinkle it with sun sachet;
Safely, Summer, store them till
You gently shake them out next May.
　　　　　　　　　　Doris Chalma Brock

Autumn

Autumn
The year's last, loveliest smile.
　　　　　　　　　　William Cullen Bryant

I saw old Autumn in the misty morn stand
shadowless like silence.
　　　　　　　　　　Thomas Hood

Winter

Winter
When Winter waves his magic wand
   A fairyland appears;
The shrubs along the picket fence
   Are knights with shining spears.

The fountain is a crystal throne
   Where old King Jack Frost rules;
The evergreens are stately queens
   In silvery lace and jewels.

The fence-post sentinels at the gate,
   Whose hats are frosty globes,
Command that all who enter here
   Be dressed in ermine robes.
Edith Powell Wortman

I looked across a vail of snow,
And there in hoods of gray
The pussy willows whisper'd low;
The Spring's not far away.
Lydia Avery Coonley

A snow year, a rich year.
George Herbert

Full knee-deep lies the winter snow, and the winter winds are wearily sighing.
Alfred Tennyson

The seasons come and go, and go and come, to teach men gratitude.
Robert Pollok

Prayer

A prayer in its simplest definition is merely a wish turned Godward.
Phillips Brooks

Not only in my summer let me sing
When Beauty storms my senses and my soul,
When mine is the mysterious and dark
Delight of one who feels the quivering
Tumultuous heart surrender utterly,
Idolatrous of that bright deity.
Let me not ever lose the moment when
I stand, transfigured, on the shining verge
Of dreams beyond all telling and I glimpse
The realm where earth and heaven
   subtly merge.
O God, when in my winter I shall walk
The quiet and the twilight ways along,
Let me feel still a breath upon my brow
And find in snow the silver seeds of song.
Adelaide Love

Prayer is the wing wherewith the soul flies to heaven, and meditation the eye wherewith we see God.
Saint Ambrose

Lord, make me an instrument of Your peace,
Where there is hatred, let me sow love;
Where there is injury, pardon;
Where there is doubt, faith;
Where there is despair, hope;
Where there is darkness, light, and
Where there is sadness, joy.

O, Divine Master, grant that I may not so much
Seek to be consoled as to console;
To be understood as to understand;
To be loved as to love;
For it is in giving that we receive;
It is in pardoning that we are pardoned;
And it is in dying that we are born to eternal life.
Saint Francis of Assisi

Prayer should be the key of the day and the lock of the night.
Thomas Fuller

Pray and hurl your life after your prayers.
Harry Emerson Fosdick

In prayer the lips ne'er act the winning part
Without the sweet concurrence of the heart.
Robert Herrick

Prayer is the world in tune.
HENRY VAUGHAN

An Indian Prayer
Grant that I may not criticize my neighbor until I have walked a mile in his moccasins.

One single grateful thought raised to heaven is a perfect prayer.
Gotthold Ephraim Lessing

The Universal Prayer

Father of all! in every age,
    In every clime adored,
By saint, by savage, and by sage,
    Jehovah, Jove, or Lord!

Thou great First Cause, least understood,
    Who all my sense confined
To know but this, that thou art good,
    And that myself am blind;

Yet gave me, in this dark estate,
    To see the good from ill;
And, binding nature fast in fate,
    Left free the human will:

What conscience dictates to be done,
    Or warns me not to do,
This, teach me more than hell to shun,
    That, more than heaven pursue.

What blessings thy free bounty gives
    Let me not cast away;
For God is paid when man receives,
    To enjoy is to obey.

Yet not to earth's contracted span
    Thy goodness let me bound,
Or think thee Lord alone of man,
    When thousand worlds are round:

Let not this weak, unknowing hand
    Presume thy bolts to throw,
And deal damnation round the land
    On each I judge thy foe.

If I am right, thy grace impart
    Still in the right to stay;
If I am wrong, O, teach my heart
    To find that better way!

Save me alike from foolish pride
    And impious discontent
At aught thy wisdom has denied,
    Or aught thy goodness lent.

Teach me to feel another's woe,
    To hide the fault I see;
That mercy I to others show,
    That mercy show to me.

Mean though I am, not wholly so,
    Since quickened by thy breath;
O, lead me wheresoe'er I go,
    Through this day's life or death!

This day be bread and peace my lot;
    All else beneath the sun,
Thou know'st if best bestowed or not,
    And let thy will be done.

To thee, whose temple is all space,
    Whose altar, earth, sea, skies,
One chorus let all Being raise,
    All Nature's incense rise!

Alexander Pope

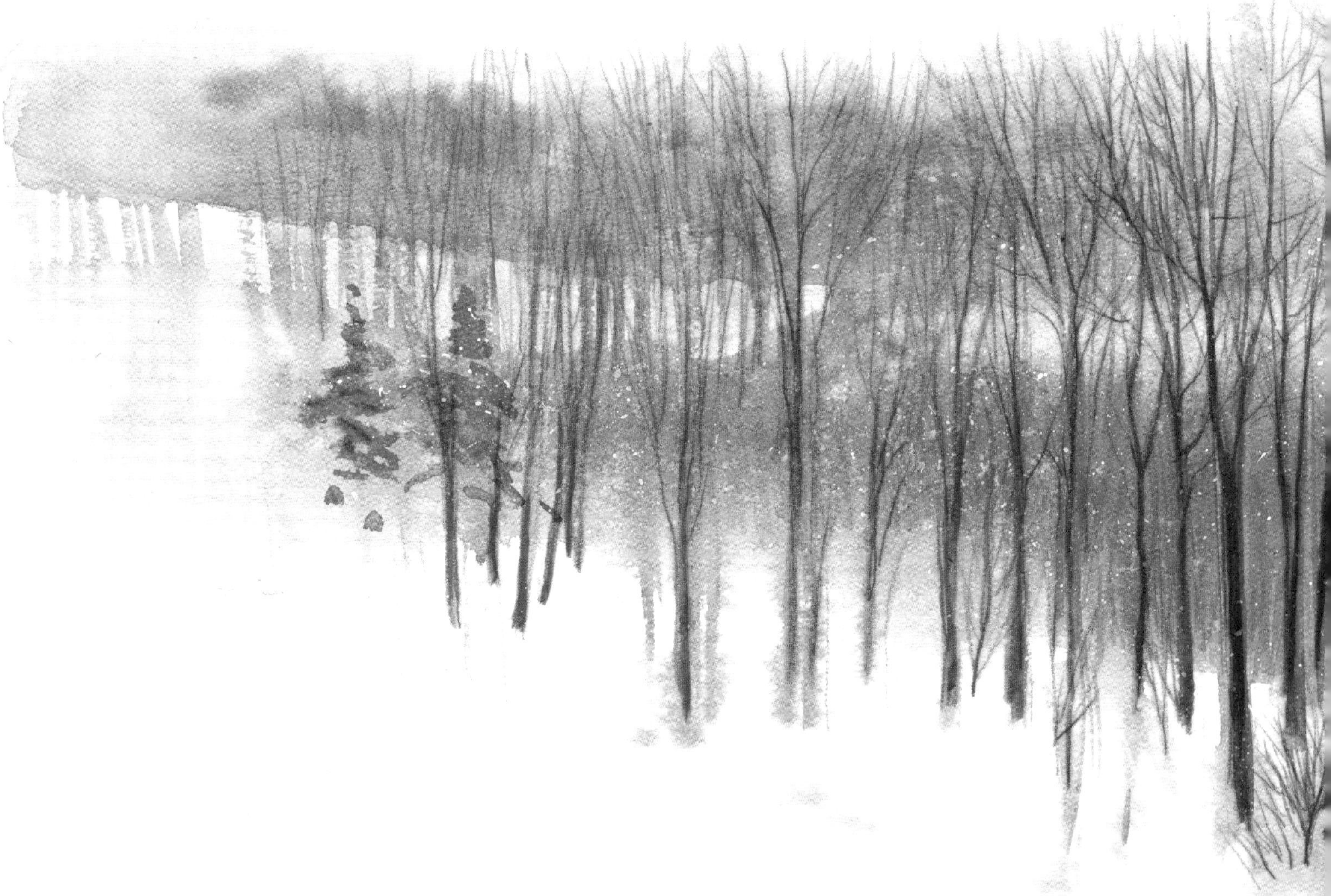

Life

Stopping by Woods on a Snowy Evening

Whose woods these are I think I know.
His house is in the village though;
He will not see me stopping here
To watch his woods fill up with snow.

My little horse must think it queer
To stop without a farmhouse near
Between the woods and frozen lake
The darkest evening of the year.

He gives his harness bells a shake
To ask if there is some mistake.
The only other sound's the sweep
Of easy wind and downy flake.

The woods are lovely, dark and deep.
But I have promises to keep,
And miles to go before I sleep,
And miles to go before I sleep.

Robert Frost

O Captain! My Captain!

O Captain! my Captain! our fearful trip is done,
The ship has weather'd every rack, the prize we sought is won,
The port is near, the bells I hear, the people all exulting,
While follow eyes the steady keel, the vessel grim and daring;
    But O heart! heart! heart!
      O the bleeding drops of red,
        Where on the deck my Captain lies,
          Fallen cold and dead.

O Captain! my Captain! rise up and hear the bells;
Rise up--for you the flag is flung--for you the bugle trills,
For you bouquets and ribbon'd wreaths--for you the shores a-crowding,
For you they call, the swaying mass, their eager faces turning;
    Here Captain! dear father!
      The arm beneath your head!
        It is some dream that on the deck,
          You've fallen cold and dead.

My Captain does not answer, his lips are pale and still,
My father does not feel my arm, he has no pulse nor will,
The ship is anchor'd safe and sound, its voyage closed and done,
From fearful trip the victor ship comes in with object won;
    Exult O shores, and ring O bells!
      But I, with mournful tread,
        Walk the deck my Captain lies,
          Fallen cold and dead.
        Walt Whitman

Oh, the Wild Joys of Living!

Oh, the wild joys of living! the leaping from rock to rock,
The strong rending of boughs from the fir-tree, the cool silver shock
Of the plunge in the pool's living water, the hunt of the bear,
And the sultriness showing the lion is couched in his lair.
And the meal, the rich dates yellowed over the gold dust divine,
And the locust-flesh steeped in the pitcher, the full draft of wine,
And the sleep in the dried river-channel where bulrushes tell
That the water was wont to go warbling so softly and well.
How good is man's life, the mere living! how fit to employ
All the heart and the soul and the senses forever in joy!
        Robert Browning

A Little Song of Life
Glad that I live am I;
That the sky is blue;
Glad for the country lanes,
And the fall of dew.

After the sun the rain,
After the rain the sun;
This is the way of life,
Till the work be done.

All that we need to do,
Be we low or high
Is to see that we grow
Nearer the sky.
Lizette Woodworth Reese

Life
Life is a gift to be used every day,
Not to be smothered and hidden away;
It isn't a thing to be stored in the chest
Where you gather your keepsakes and
   treasure your best;
It isn't a joy to be sipped now and then
And promptly put back in a dark
   place again.

Life is a gift that the humblest may boast of
And one that the humblest may well make
   the most of.
Get out and live it each hour of the day,
Wear it and use it as much as you may;
Don't keep it in niches and corners
   and grooves,
You'll find that in service its
   beauty improves.
Edgar A. Guest

The glory of life comes not from the things we can command *but* from the things we can reverence.
Anonymous

May you live as long as you like, and love all you like as long as you live.
Anonymous

Life is a leaf of paper white
Whereon each one of us may write.
James Russell Lowell

The Village Blacksmith

Under a spreading chestnut-tree
   The village smithy stands;
The smith, a mighty man is he,
   With large and sinewy hands;
And the muscles of his brawny arms
   Are strong as iron bands.

His hair is crisp and black and long;
   His face is like the tan;
His brow is wet with honest sweat,
   He earns whate'er he can
And looks the whole world in the face,
   For he owes not any man.

Week in, week out, from morn till night,
   You can hear his bellows blow;
You can hear him swing his heavy sledge,
   With measured beat and slow,
Like a sexton ringing the village bell
   When the evening sun is low.

And children coming home from school
   Look in at the open door;
They love to see the flaming forge
   And hear the bellows roar
And catch the burning sparks that fly
   Like chaff from the threshing-floor.

He goes on Sunday to the church
   And sits among his boys;
He hears the parson pray and preach;
   He hears his daughter's voice
Singing in the village choir,
   And it makes his heart rejoice.

It sounds to him like her mother's voice,
   Singing in Paradise!
He needs must think of her once more,
   How in the grave she lies;
And with his hard, rough hand he wipes
   A tear out of his eyes.

Toiling, rejoicing, sorrowing,
   Onward through life he goes;
Each morning sees some task begin,
   Each evening sees it close;
Something attempted, something done
   Has earned a night's repose.

Thanks, thanks to thee, my worthy friend,
   For the lesson thou hast taught!
Thus at the flaming forge of life
   Our fortunes must be wrought;
Thus on its sounding anvil shaped
   Each burning deed and thought!

Henry Wadsworth Longfellow

Splendid Gift

Live your life while you have it. Life is a splendid gift. There is nothing small in it. For the greatest things grow by God's Law out of the smallest. But to live your life you must discipline it. You must not fritter it away in "fair purpose, erring act, inconstant will" but make your thoughts, your acts, all work to the same end and that end, not self but God.

That is what we call character.
Florence Nightingale

We are life...
...and life is us!
PETER SEYMOUR

The Mystery of Life

We had sat beside the little pool and watched the tree frogs and the horsehair worms and the waterskaters, and had wondered how they got there, so far from other water. It seemed to us that life in every form is incipiently everywhere waiting for a chance to take root and start reproducing; eggs, spores, seeds, bacilli--everywhere. Let a raindrop fall and it is crowded with the waiting life. Everything is everywhere; and we, seeing the desert country, the hot waterless expanse, and knowing how far away the nearest water must be, say with a kind of disbelief, "How did they get clear here, these little animals?" And until we can attack with our poor blunt weapon of reason that causal process and reduce it, we do not quite believe in the horsehair worms and the tree frogs. The great fact is that they are there. Seeing a school of fish lying quietly in still water, all the heads pointing in one direction, one says, "It is unusual that this is so"--but it isn't unusual at all. We begin at the wrong end. They simply lie that way, and it is remarkable only because with our blunt tool we cannot carve out a human reason. Everything is potentially everywhere--the body is potentially cancerous, phthisic, strong to resist or weak to receive. In one swing of the balance the waiting life pounces in and takes possession and grows strong while our own individual chemistry is distorted past the point where it can maintain its balance. This we call dying, and by the process we do not give nor offer but are taken by a multiform life and used for its proliferation. These things are balanced A man is potentially all things too, greedy and cruel, capable of great love or great hatred, of balanced or unbalanced so-called emotions. This is the way he is--one factor in a surge of striving. And he continues to ask "why" without first admitting to himself his cosmic identity.
John Steinbeck

LIFE

One way to get the most out of life is to look upon it as an adventure.
William Feather

Life can only be understood backwards; but it must be lived forwards.
Soren Kierkegaard

Every man's life is a fairy tale, written by God's fingers.
Hans Christian Andersen

...Life is the *love* that reaches out...
   ...building bridges across gulfs of
     uncertainty...
    ...to touch
      hands
       hearts
        souls...
...in the experience of union.
Peter Seymour

Look to this day!
For it is life, the very life of life.
In its brief course lie all the verities
   and realities of your existence:
The bliss of growth;
The glory of action;
The splendor of beauty;
For yesterday is already a dream,
   and tomorrow is only a vision;
But today, well lived, makes every yesterday
A dream of happiness, and every tomorrow
   a vision of hope.
Look well, therefore, to this day!
from the Sanskrit

Kindness

How beautiful a day can be when kindness touches it.

George Elliston

KINDNESS

Kind words produce their own image in men's souls; and a beautiful image it is. They soothe and quiet and comfort the hearer. They shame him out of his sour, morose, unkind feelings. We have not yet begun to use kind words in such abundance as they ought to be used.

Blaise Pascal

Loving-kindness is the better part of goodness. It lends grace to the sterner qualities of which this consists and makes it a little less difficult to practice those minor virtues of self-control and self-restraint, patience, discipline and tolerance, which are the passive and not very exhilarating elements of goodness. Goodness is the only value that seems in this world of appearances to have any claim to be an end in itself. Virtue is its own reward. I am ashamed to have reached so commonplace a conclusion. With my instinct for effect I should have liked to end…with some startling and paradoxical announcement or with a cynicism that my readers would have recognized with a chuckle as characteristic. It seems I have little more to say than can be read in any copybook or heard from any pulpit. I have gone a long way round to discover what everyone knew already.

W. Somerset Maugham

The greatest pleasure I know is to do a good action by stealth and to have it found out by accident.

Charles Lamb

He who sows courtesy reaps friendship, and he who plants kindness gathers love.

Richard Brooks

Paradise is open to all kind hearts.

Pierre Jean de Béranger

Kindness in words creates confidence, kindness in thinking creates profoundness, kindness in giving creates love.

Lao-Tse

The happiness of life may be greatly increased by small courtesies in which there is no parade, whose voice is too still to tease, and which manifest themselves by tender and affectionate looks and little kind acts of attention.

Lawrence Sterne

A kind heart is a fountain of gladness, making everything in its vicinity freshen into smiles.

Washington Irving

The whole worth of a kind deed lies in the love that inspires it.

from the Talmud

The heart of the giver makes the gift dear and precious.

Martin Luther

Do all the good you can,
By all the means you can,
In all the ways you can,
In all the places you can,
At all the times you can,
To all the people you can,
As long as ever you can.

John Wesley

Nature

Let man then contemplate the whole of nature in her full and grand majesty, and turn his vision from the low objects which surround him. Let him gaze on that brilliant light, set like an eternal lamp to illumine the universe; let the earth appear to him a point in comparison with the vast circle described by the sun; and let him wonder at the fact that this vast circle is itself but a very fine point in comparison with that described by the stars in their revolution round the firmament. But if our view be arrested there, let our imagination pass beyond; it will sooner exhaust the power of conception than nature that of supplying material for conception. The whole visible world is only an imperceptible atom in the ample bosom of nature. No idea approaches it. We may enlarge our conceptions beyond all imaginable space; we only produce atoms in comparison with the reality of things. It is an infinite sphere, the centre of which is everywhere, the circumference nowhere. In short it is the greatest sensible mark of the almighty power of God, that imagination loses itself in that thought….

What is man in nature? A Nothing in comparison with the Infinite, an All in comparison with the Nothing, a mean between nothing and everything. Since he is infinitely removed from comprehending the extremes, the end of things and their beginning are hopelessly hidden from him in an impenetrable secret; he is equally incapable of seeing the Nothing from which he was made, and the Infinite in which he is swallowed up….

All things proceed from the Nothing and are borne towards the Infinite. Who will follow these marvellous processes? The Author of these wonders understands them. None other can do so.

Blaise Pascal

When the Mist Rises
Along the upper reaches of the Ohio, where the foothills of the Allegheny Mountains hem in one of America's beautiful streams, you sometimes awake at daybreak to find that a heavy mist has obliterated the landscape, leaving only a narrow circle of it dimly visible about you. When this happens, you may resign yourself to the weather and wait for a change, or you may do what you have on hand with the best cheer you can muster, calling to the neighbor whose shadowy form you can see, though you cannot be sure what he is at.

As you keep busy, the mist rises. You see the river, rolling on toward the Mississippi. Then you see the opposite shore, the houses of the city, the taller buildings, the towers of the schools, the steeples of the churches, highest of all. Slowly the mist climbs the hills, hangs for a little like a torn veil on their summit, then vanishes, disclosing a blue sky. And the work you began in the fog you continue in the sunlight.
Max Otto

Nature is man's teacher. She unfolds her treasures to his search, unseals his eye, illumines his mind, and purifies his heart; an influence breathes from all the sights and sounds of her existence.
Alfred B. Street

Let us a little permit Nature to take her own way; she better understands her own affairs than we.
Michel de Montaigne

To Every Thing There Is a Season
To every thing there is a season, and a time to every purpose under the heaven:

A time to be born, and a time to die; a time to plant, and a time to pluck up that which is planted; A time to kill, and a time to heal; a time to break down, and a time to build up;

A time to weep, and a time to laugh; a time to mourn, and a time to dance; a time to cast away stones, and a time to gather stones together; a time to embrace, and a time to refrain from embracing;

A time to get, and a time to lose; a time to keep, and a time to cast away; a time to rend, and a time to sew; a time to keep silence, and a time to speak;

A time to love, and a time to hate; a time of war, and a time of peace.
Ecclesiastes 3:1-8

Nature is visible thought.

HEINRICH HEINE

To a Waterfowl

    Whither, midst falling dew,
While glow the heavens with the last steps of day,
Far, through their rosy depths, dost thou pursue
    Thy solitary way?

    Vainly the fowler's eye
Might mark thy distant flight to do thee wrong,
As, darkly seen against the crimson sky,
    Thy figure floats along.

    Seek'st thou the plashy brink
Of weedy lake, or marge of river wide,
Or where the rocking billows rise and sink
    On the chafed ocean-side?

    There is a Power whose care
Teaches thy way along that pathless coast--
The desert and illimitable air--
    Lone wandering, but not lost.

    All day thy wings have fanned,
At that far height, the cold, thin atmosphere,
Yet stoop not, weary, to the welcome land,
    Though the dark night is near.

    And soon that toil shall end;
Soon shalt thou find a summer home, and rest,
And scream among thy fellows; reeds shall bend,
    Soon, o'er thy sheltered nest.

    Thou'rt gone, the abyss of heaven
Hath swallowed up thy form; yet, on my heart
Deeply has sunk the lesson thou hast given,
    And shall not soon depart.

    He who, from zone to zone,
Guides through the boundless sky thy certain flight,
In the long way that I must tread alone,
    Will lead my steps aright.

William Cullen Bryant

The man who can really, in living union of the mind and heart, converse with God through nature finds in the material forms around him a source of power and happiness inexhaustible and like the life of angels.--The highest life and glory of man is to be alive unto God; and when this grandeur of sensibility to him and this power of communion with him is carried as the habit of the soul into the forms of nature, then the walls of our world are as the gates of heaven.
George B. Cheever

Trees
I think that I shall never see
A poem lovely as a tree.

A tree whose hungry mouth is pressed
Against the earth's sweet flowing breast;

A tree that looks at God all day
And lifts her leafy arms to pray;

A tree that may in summer wear
A nest of robins in her hair;

Upon whose bosom snow has lain;
Who intimately lives with rain.

Poems are made by fools like me,
But only God can make a tree.
Joyce Kilmer

The Love of Nature
The love of nature is ever returned double to us, not only (as) the delighter in our delight, but by linking our sweetest, but of themselves perishable, feelings to distinct and vivid images, which we ourselves, at times, and which a thousand casual recollections recall to our memory. She is the preserver, the treasurer, of our joys. Even in sickness and nervous diseases she has peopled our imagination with lovely forms, which have sometimes overpowered the inward pain and brought with them their old sensations. And even when all men have seemed to desert us, and the friend of our heart has passed on with one glance from his "cold disliking eye--" yet even then the blue heaven spreads itself out and bends over us, and the little tree still shelters us under its plumage as a second cope, a domestic firmament, and the low creeping gale will sigh in the heath plant and soothe us by sound of sympathy, till the lulled grief lose itself in fixed gaze on the purple heath-blossom, till the present beauty becomes a vision of memory.
Samuel Taylor Coleridge

*One touch of nature
makes the whole world kin.*

WILLIAM SHAKESPEARE

That man, I think, has had a liberal education, who has been so trained in youth that his body is the ready servant of his will, and does with ease and pleasure all the work that, as a mechanism, it is capable of; whose intellect is a clear, cold, logic engine, with all its parts of equal strength, and in smooth working order; ready, like a steam engine, to be turned to any kind of work, and spin the gossamers as well as forge the anchors of the mind; whose mind is stored with a knowledge of the great and fundamental truths of Nature and of the laws of her operations; one who, no stunted ascetic, is full of life and fire, but whose passions are trained to come to heel by a vigorous will, the servant of a tender conscience; who has learned to love all beauty, whether of Nature or of art, to hate all vileness, and to respect others as himself.

Such an one, and no other, I conceive, has had a liberal education; for he is, as completely as a man can be, in harmony with Nature. He will make the best of her, and she of him. They will get on together rarely; she as his ever beneficent mother; he as her mouthpiece, her conscious self, her minister and interpreter.

Thomas H. Huxley

Lines Written in Early Spring
I heard a thousand blended notes,
While in a grove I sate reclined,
In that sweet mood when pleasant thoughts
Bring sad thoughts to the mind.

To her fair works did Nature link
The human soul that through me ran;
And much it grieved my heart to think
What man has made of man.

Through primrose tufts, in that green bower,
The periwinkle trailed its wreaths;
And 'tis my faith that every flower
Enjoys the air it breathes.

The birds around me hopped and played,
Their thoughts I cannot measure:--
But the least motion which they made
It seemed a thrill of pleasure.

The budding twigs spread out their fan
To catch the breezy air;
And I must think, do all I can,
That there was pleasure there.

If this belief from heaven be sent,
If such be Nature's holy plan,
Have I not reason to lament
What man has made of man?

William Wordsworth

All are but parts of one stupendous whole,
Whose body Nature is, and God the soul;
That, chang'd thro' all, and yet in all the same;
Great in the earth, as in th' ethereal frame;
Warms in the sun, refreshes in the breeze,
Glows in the stars, and blossoms in the trees,
Lives thro' all life, extends thro' all extent,
Spreads undivided, operates unspent;
Breathes in our soul, informs our mortal part,
As full, as perfect, in a hair as heart;
As full, as perfect, in vile Man that mourns,
As the rapt Seraph that adores and burns;
To him no high, no low, no great, no small;
He fills, he bounds, connects, and equals all.
Alexander Pope

There is a pleasure in the pathless woods,
There is rapture on the lonely shore,
There is society where none intrudes,
By the deep sea, and music in its roar;
I love not man the less, but Nature more.
Lord Byron

Nature is the art of God.
Sir Thomas Browne

from Nature Lover's Creed
My creed is: Stars,
    And wild birds flying,
October winds
    And hills low-lying;

The late March snows
    And April's waking,
With orchard trees
    Their pink wealth shaking;

A red-brown road
    From towns far leading
Through vistas wide--
    Old cares unheeding;

A plain, sweet hut
    By meadows waiting
For hearts grown tired
    Of human hating;

Old-fashioned flowers,
    And rains light-tapping;
Wide, sandy shores,
    And bright waves lapping.

So here's my creed--
    And how I love it!--
Beauty in earth,
    And God above it.
Thomas Curtis Clark

The Voice
The voice that beautifies the soil!
The voice on high,
The voice of rolling thunder,
Above the darkening clouds
Again and again it is heard,
The voice that beautifies the soil!
Navajo Chant

Misty
The mist looks down
With gentle eye
And tenderly,
While passing by,
Lightly reaches out her hand
To smooth the wrinkles
Of the land.
Doris Chalma Brock

He is made one with nature:
There is heard
His voice in all her music,
From the moan
Of thunder to the song of
Night's sweet bird.
Percy Bysshe Shelley

Youth

The Barefoot Boy

Blessings on thee, little man,
Barefoot boy, with cheek of tan!
With thy turned-up pantaloons,
And thy merry whistled tunes;
With thy red lip, redder still,
Kissed by strawberries on the hill;
With the sunshine on thy face,
Through thy torn brim's jaunty grace,
From my heart I give thee joy--
I was once a barefoot boy.
Prince thou art--the grown-up man
Only is republican;
Let the million-dollared ride!
Barefoot, trudging at his side,
Thou hast more than he can buy,
In the reach of ear and eye--
Outward sunshine, inward joy;
Blessings on thee, barefoot boy!
          John Greenleaf Whittier

Mighty things from small beginnings grow.
John Dryden

In youth the heart exults and sings,
The pulses leap, the feet have wings.
Henry Wadsworth Longfellow

Build sure in the beginning.
James Russell Lowell

Youth comes but once in a lifetime.
Henry Wadsworth Longfellow

Youth! youth! how buoyant are thy hopes!
They turn,
Like marigolds, toward the sunny side.
Jean Ingelow

The thoughts of youth are long,
long thoughts.
Henry Wadsworth Longfellow

There is no age, for youth is the divine....
Eva Gore-Booth

My youth is but a summer's day,
Then like the bee and ant I'll lay
   A store of learning by;
And though from flower to flower I rove,
My stock of wisdom I'll improve,
   Nor be a butterfly.
Amy Brooks

Youth is a poem
With a springtime theme,
Measured by moments
Of laughter and dreams.

Youth is a melody,
Vibrant and clear,
That will echo in memory
Year after year.

Youth is a portrait,
Proud and free,
With eyes that reflect
The promise they see.

Youth is a garden,
Bright with flowers,
To twine round the strength
Of tomorrow's towers.
George D. Walley

For a Child
Your friends shall be the tall wind,
   The river and the tree,
The sun that laughs and marches,
   The swallow and the sea.

Your prayers shall be the murmur
   Of grasses in the rain,
The song of wildwood thrushes
   That makes God glad again.

And you shall run and wander,
   And you shall dream and sing
Of brave things and bright things
   Beyond the swallow's wing.

And you shall envy no man,
   Nor hurt your heart with sighs,
For I will keep you simple
   That God may make you wise.
Fanny Stearns Davis

O youth, whose hope is high,
Who dost to Truth aspire,
Whether thou live or die,
O look not back nor tire.
Robert Bridges

The Old Oaken Bucket

How dear to my heart are the scenes of my childhood,
    When fond recollection presents them to view!
The orchard, the meadow, the deep tangled wildwood,
    And every loved spot which my infancy knew,
The wide-spreading pond and the mill that stood by it,
    The bridge and the rock where the cataract fell;
The cot of my father, the dairy house nigh it,
    And e'en the rude bucket that hung in the well.

That moss-covered bucket I hailed as a treasure,
    For often at noon, when returned from the field,
I found it the source of an exquisite pleasure,
    The purest and sweetest that nature can yield.
How ardent I seized it, with hands that were glowing,
    And quick to the white-pebbled bottom it fell.
Then soon, with the emblem of truth overflowing,
    And dripping with coolness, it rose from the well.

How sweet from the green, mossy brim to receive it,
    As, poised on the curb, it inclined to my lips!
Not a full, blushing goblet could tempt me to leave it,
    Tho' filled with the nectar that Jupiter sips.
And now, far removed from the loved habitation,
    The tear of regret will intrusively swell,
As fancy reverts to my father's plantation
    And sighs for the bucket that hung in the well.
                Samuel Woodworth

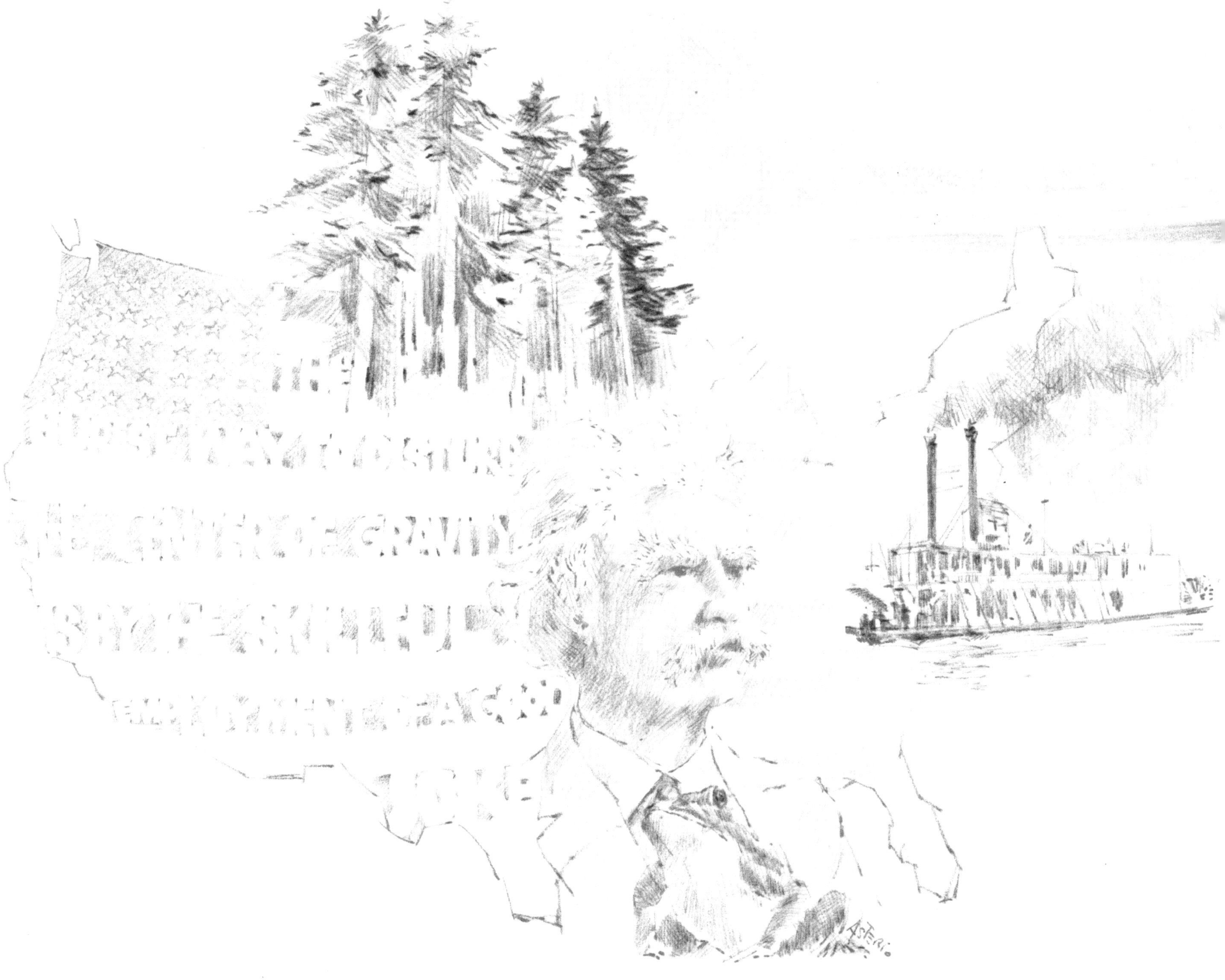

Laughter

American Laughter

Oh the men who laughed the American laughter
Whittled their jokes from the fresh tree-pines;
They were tall men, sharpened before and after;
They studied the sky for the weather-signs;
They tilted their hats and they smoked long-nines.

Their laughter was ladled in Western flagons
And poured down throats that were parched for more;
This was the laughter of democrat-wagons
And homely men at the crossroads store
--It tickled the shawl that a lawyer wore!

It hurt the ears of the dainty and pretty
But they laughed the louder and laughed their fill,
A laughter made for Virginia City,
Springfield, and Natchez-under-the-Hill,
And the river that flows past Hannibal still!

American laughter was lucky laughter,
A coonskin tune by a homespun bard;
It tasted of hams from the smokehouse rafter
And locust trees in the courthouse yard,
And Petroleum Nasby and Artemus Ward!

They laughed at the Mormons and Mike Fink's daughter
And the corncob tale of Sut Lovingood's dog,
Till the ague fled from the fever-water
And the damps deserted the tree-stump bog,
--They laughed at the tale of the jumping frog!

They laughed at the British, they laughed at the Shakers,
At Horace Greeley and stovepipe hats;
They split their fences and plowed their acres,
And treed their troubles like mountain cats;
--They laughed calamity out of the flats!

Now the Boston man, according to rumor,
Said, as he turned in his high-backed bed,
"This doesn't conform to my rules for humor,"
And he settled his night cap over his head,
--But it shook the earth like the buffalo tread!

And the corn grew tall and the fields grew wider,
And the land grew sleek with the mirth they sowed;
They laughed the fat meat into the spider,
They laughed the blues from the Wilderness Road,
--They crossed hard times to the Comstock Lode!

Kenneth Allan Robinson

LAUGHTER

Mirth is God's medicine.
Henry Ward Beecher

Laughter is a man's friend, for it lightens all his burdens.
O. Blumenthal

At Day's End
Laughter, like gay ribbons,
  Drifts where children play,
And with its happy streamers
  I bind my lovely day!
Emily Carey Alleman

…God hath made me to laugh, so that all that hear will laugh with me.
Genesis 21:6

A day is wasted without laughter.
Nicolas Chamfort

Laughter is the sensation of feeling good all over and showing it principally in one spot.
Josh Billings

The good life is the healthful life, the merry life. Life is health, joy, laughter. There is much disease and chaos and ugliness in the world. Yet is there a stream of love, of health and beauty-making power, flowing through the all. This is the sap and inspiration of creation….

There is the laughter which is born out of the pure joy of living, the spontaneous expression of health and energy — the sweet laughter of the child. This is a gift of God. There is the warm laughter of the kindly soul which heartens the discouraged, gives health to the sick and comfort to the dying…. There is, above all, the laughter that comes from the eternal joy of creation, the joy of making the world new, the joy of expressing the inner riches of the soul — laughter that triumphs over pain and hardship in the passion for an enduring ideal, the joy of bringing the light of happiness, of truth and beauty into a dark world. This is divine laughter par excellence.
J. E. Bodin

I like the laughter that opens the lips and the heart, that shows at the same time pearls and the soul.
Victor Hugo

To laugh often and much: to win the respect of intelligent people and affection of children; to earn the appreciation of honest critics and endure the betrayal of false friends; to appreciate beauty, to find the best in others; to leave the world a bit better, whether by a healthy child, a garden patch or a redeemed social condition; to know even one life has breathed easier because you have lived. This is to have succeeded.
Ralph Waldo Emerson

A good laugh is sunshine in a house.

WILLIAM MAKEPEACE THACKERAY

Age

Old age, on tiptoe, lays her jeweled hand
Lightly in mine.--Come, tread a stately measure,
Most gracious partner, nobly posed and bland.
    Ours be no boisterous pleasure,
But smiling conversation, with quick glance
And memories dancing lightlier than we dance,
    Friends who a thousand joys
Divide and double, save one joy supreme
    Which many a pang alloys.
    Let wanton girls and boys
Cry over lovers' woes and broken toys.
Our waking life is sweeter than their dream.

Dame Nature, with unwitting hand,
Has sparsely strewn the black abyss with lights
Minute, remote, and numberless. We stand
    Measuring far depths and heights,
    Arched over by a laughing heaven,
Intangible and never to be scaled.
If we confess our sins, they are forgiven.
    We triumph, if we know we failed.
Tears that in youth you shed,
Congealed to pearls, now deck your silvery hair;
    Sighs breathed for love long dead
Frosted the glittering atoms of the air
    Into the veils you wear
Round your soft bosom and most queenly head;
    The shimmer of your gown
Catches all tints of autumn, and the dew
Of gardens where the damask roses blew;

The myriad tapers from these arches hung
    Play on your diamonded crown;
And stars, whose light angelical caressed
    Your virgin days,
Give back in your calm eyes their holier rays.
    The deep past living in your breast
    Heaves these half-merry sighs;
    And the soft accents of your tongue
    Breathe unrecorded charities.

    Hasten not; the feast will wait.
This is a master-night without a morrow.
No chill and haggard dawn, with after-sorrow,
    Will snuff the spluttering candle out,
Or blanch the revellers homeward straggling late
    Before the rout
Wearies or wanes, will come a calmer trance.
Lulled by the poppied fragrance of this bower,
    We'll cheat the lapsing hour,
And close our eyes, still smiling, on the dance.

George Santayana

AGE

To Age

Welcome, old friend! These many years
    Have we lived door by door:
The Fates have laid aside their shears
    Perhaps for some few more.

I was indocile at an age
    When better boys were taught,
But thou at length hast made me sage,
    If I am sage in aught.

Little I know from other men,
    Too little they from me,
But thou hast pointed well the pen
    That writes these lines to thee.

Thanks for expelling Fear and Hope,
    One vile, the other vain;
One's scourge, the other's telescope,
    I shall not see again:

Rather what lies before my feet
    My notice shall engage--
He who hath braved Youth's dizzy heat
    Dreads not the frost of Age.
        Walter Savage Landor

The evening of a well-spent life brings its lamps with it.
    Joseph Joubert

The human heart, at whatever age, opens only to the heart that opens in return.
    Maria Edgeworth

No Spring, no Summer beauty hath such grace,
As I have seen in an Autumnal face.
    John Donne

You'll find as you grow older that you weren't born such a very great while ago after all. The time shortens up.
    William Dean Howells

No wise man ever wished to be younger.
    Swift

Grow old along with me!
    The best is yet to be,
The last of life, for which the first was made:
    Our times are in His hand
    Who saith "A whole I planned,
Youth shows but half; trust God: see all, nor be afraid!"
    Robert Browning

Wrinkles should merely indicate where smiles have been.
    Mark Twain

As a white candle
    In a holy place
So is the beauty
    Of an aged face.
    Joseph Campbell

The autumn of the beautiful is beautiful.
    Latin Proverb

Gray hairs seem to my fancy like the soft light of the moon, silvering over the evening of life.
    Jean Paul Richter

The Later Years
The present is a fleeting moment, the past is no more; and our prospect of futurity is dark and doubtful. This day may possibly be my last; but the laws of probability, so true in general, so fallacious in particular, still allow me about fifteen years, and I shall soon enter into the period which, as the most agreeable of his long life, was selected by the judgment and experience of the sage Fontenelle. His choice is approved by the eloquent historian of Nature, who fixes our moral happiness to the mature season in which our passions are supposed to be calmed, our duties fulfilled, our ambition satisfied, and our fame and fortune established on a solid basis. In private conversation, that great and amiable man added the weight of his own experience; and this autumnal felicity might be exemplified in the lives of Voltaire, Hume, and many other men of letters. I am far more inclined to embrace than dispute this comfortable doctrine. I will not suppose any premature decay of the mind or body; but I must reluctantly observe that two causes, the abbreviation of time and the failure of hope, will always tinge with a browner shade the evening of life.
-Autobiography

Edward Gibbon

I am still at work, with my hand to the plow, and my face to the future. The shadows of evening lengthen about me, but morning is in my heart. I have lived from the forties of one century to the thirties of the next. I have had varied fields of labor, and full contact with men and things, and have warmed both hands before the fire of life.

The testimony I bear is this: that the Castle of Enchantment is not yet behind me. It is before me still, and daily I catch glimpses of its battlements and towers. The rich spoils of memory are mine. Mine, too, are the precious things of today-- books, flowers, pictures, nature, and sport. The first of May is still an enchanted day to me. The best thing of all is friends. The best of life is always further on. Its real lure is hidden from our eyes, somewhere behind the hills of time.

Sir William Mulock

Calm days,
The swift years
Forgotten.

TAIGI

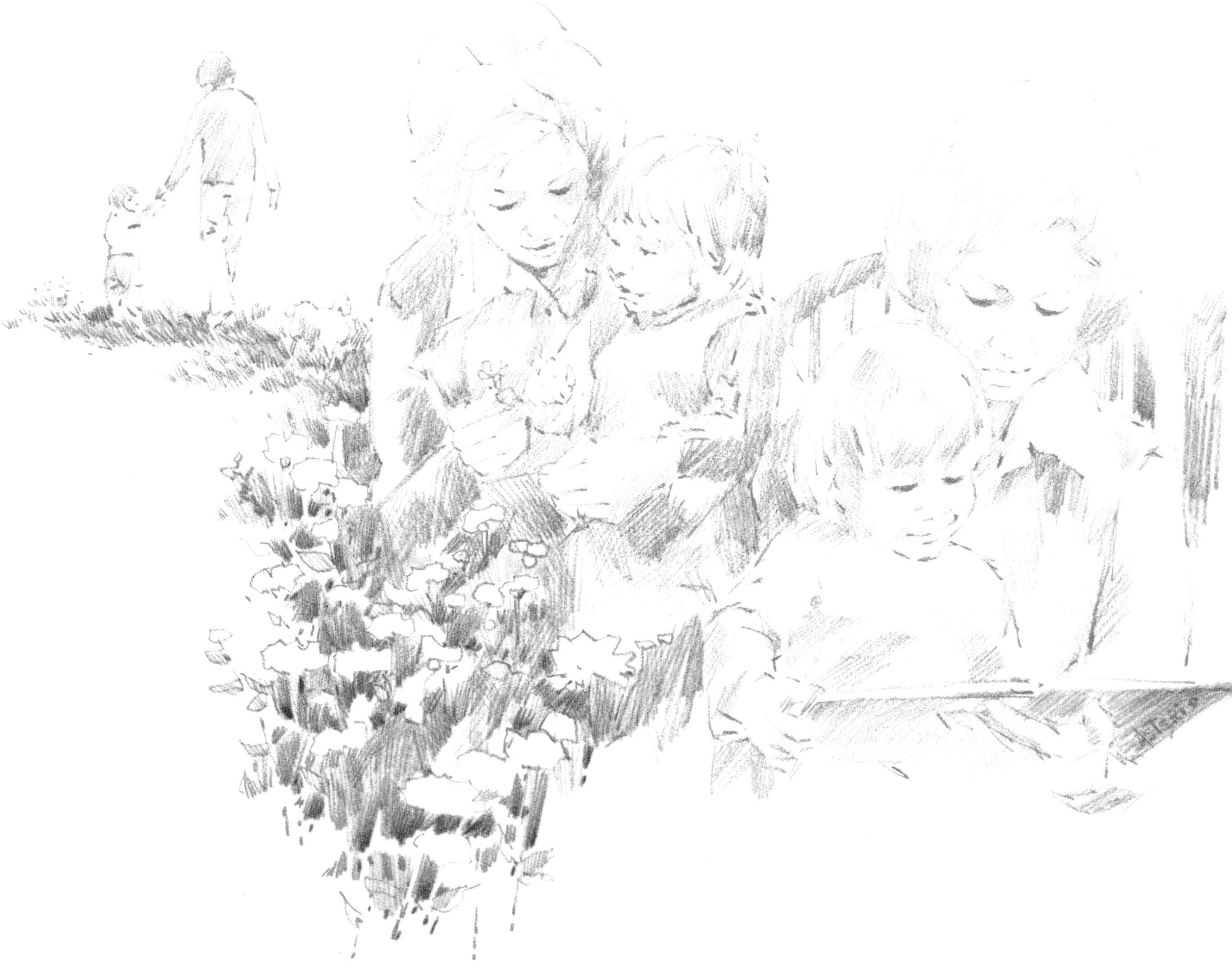

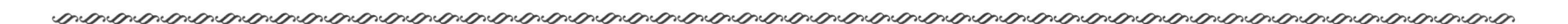

Motherhood

Why God Made Mothers

God knew that everybody needs
Someone to show the way,
He knew that babies need someone
To care for them each day…
He knew they needed someone sweet
To soothe their baby cries,
To teach them how to walk and talk
And sing them lullabies…
That's why God made mothers.

He knew small children need someone
To lend a guiding hand,
To answer all their questions
And to smile and understand,
Someone to read them storybooks,
To teach them wrong from right,
To show them wonderful new games
And hear their prayers at night…
That's why God made mothers.

And then throughout their childhood years,
God knew that children need
Someone to smile at them with pride,
Encourage each new deed.
As they grow up and all their lives,
God knew that everywhere
All children need a mother's heart
To understand and care,
And that's why God made mothers.

Katherine Nelson Davis

MOTHERHOOD

To Mother
Sweet and Low
Sweet and low, sweet and low,
   Wind of the western sea,
Low, low, breathe and blow,
   Wind of the western sea!
Over the rolling waters go,
Come from the dying moon and blow,
   Blow him again to me;
While my little one, while my pretty one,
   sleeps.

Sleep and rest, sleep and rest,
   Father will come to thee soon;
Rest, rest, on mother's breast,
   Father will come to thee soon;
Father will come to his babe in the nest,
Silver sails all out of the west
   Under the silver moon;
Sleep, my little one, sleep, my pretty one,
   sleep.
Alfred Tennyson

Motherhood
Womanliness means only motherhood;
All love begins and ends there--
   roams enough,
But, having run the circle, rests at home.
Robert Browning

Mother
…The angels, whispering to one another,
Can find, among their burning terms of love,
None so devotional as that of "Mother"….
Edgar Allan Poe

Because She Is a Mother
She broke the bread into two fragments and gave them to the children, who ate with avidity. "She hath kept none for herself," grumbled the sergeant. "Because she is not hungry," said a soldier. "Because she is a mother," said the sergeant.
Victor Hugo

Youth fades; love droops; the leaves
   of friendship fall:
A mother's secret love outlives them all.
Oliver Wendell Holmes

I would weave you a song, my mother,…
Yours the tender hand Upon my breast;
Yours the voice Sounding ever in my ears.
Madeleine Mason-Manheim

Who ran to help me, when I fell
And would some pretty story tell
Or kiss the place to make it well?
   My Mother.
Ann Taylor

When God thought of mother,
He must have laughed with satisfaction
and framed it quickly--
so rich, so deep, so divine,
so full of soul, power and beauty
was the conception.
Henry Ward Beecher

The real religion of the world comes from women much more than from men--from mothers most of all, who carry the key of our souls in their bosoms.
Oliver Wendell Holmes

The parental love which fills a woman's heart when she holds her little child in her arms, as even we childless ones must see, is something so divine, so pure from all selfishness, where it is felt aright, that every care and fatigue and sacrifice comes to the mother as a matter of course.
Frances Power Cobbe

Mother o' Mine
If I were hanged on the highest hill,
   Mother o' mine, O mother o' mine!
I know whose love would follow me still,
   Mother o' mine, O mother o' mine!

If I were drowned in the deepest sea,
   Mother o' mine, O mother o' mine!
I know whose tears would come down to me,
   Mother o' mine, O mother o' mine!

If I were damned of body and soul,
I know whose prayers would make me whole,
   Mother o' mine, O mother o' mine!
Rudyard Kipling

The sweetest sounds to mortals given
Are heard in Mother, Home and Heaven.
William Goldsmith Brown

God could not be everywhere and therefore he made mothers.
A Jewish Proverb

Where there is a mother in the house, matters speed well.
Amos Bronson Alcott

All that I am or hope to be, I owe to my angel mother.
Abraham Lincoln

For when you looked into my mother's eyes, you knew, as if He had told you, why God sent her into the world-- it was to open the minds of all who looked, to beautiful thoughts.
Sir James M. Barrie

All that I am my mother made me.
John Quincy Adams

To Mother
I learned love that is not troublesome;
   Whose service is my special dignity,
And she my guiding star while I go
   and come.

And so because you love me, and because
   I love you, Mother, I have woven
     a wreath
   Of rhymes wherewith to crown your
     honored name:
   In you not fourscore years can dim
     the flame
Of love, whose blessed glow transcends
   the laws
   Of time and change and mortal life
     and death.
Christina G. Rossetti

What Is a Mother?

A mother can be almost any size or any age, but she won't admit to anything over thirty. A mother has soft hands and smells good. A mother likes new dresses, music, a clean house, her children's kisses, an automatic washer and Daddy.

A mother doesn't like having her children sick, muddy feet, temper tantrums, loud noise or bad report cards. A mother can read a thermometer (much to the amazement of Daddy) and, like magic, can kiss a hurt away.

A mother can bake good cakes and pies but likes to see her children eat vegetables. A mother can stuff a fat baby into a snowsuit in seconds and can kiss sad little faces and make them smile.

A mother is underpaid, has long hours and gets very little rest. She worries too much about her children but she says she doesn't mind at all. And no matter how old her children are, she still likes to think of them as her little babies.

She is the guardian angel of the family, the queen, the tender hand of love. A mother is the best friend anyone ever has. A mother is love.

Anonymous

The Picture

The painter has with his brush transferred the landscape to the canvas with such fidelity that the trees and grasses seem almost real; he has made even the face of a maiden seem instinct with life, but there is one picture so beautiful that no painter has ever been able perfectly to reproduce it, and that is the picture of the mother holding in her arms her babe.

William Jennings Bryan

The many make the household, but only one the home.

JAMES RUSSELL LOWELL

She Shall Be Praised

Who can find a virtuous woman? for her price is far above rubies.

Strength and honour are her clothing; and she shall rejoice in time to come.

She openeth her mouth with wisdom; and in her tongue is the law of kindness.

She looketh well to the ways of her household, and eateth not the bread of idleness.

Her children arise up, and call her blessed; her husband also, and he praiseth her.

Many daughters have done virtuously, but thou excellest them all.

Favour is deceitful, and beauty is vain: but a woman that feareth the Lord, she shall be praised.

Give her of the fruit of her hands; and let her own works praise her in the gates.

Proverbs 31:10, 25-31

To Mother

Her household motions light and free,
And steps of virgin liberty;
A countenance in which did meet
Sweet records, promises as sweet;
A creature not too bright or good
For human nature's daily food,
For transient sorrows, simple wiles,
Praise, blame, love, kisses, tears, and smiles.

And now I see with eye serene
The very pulse of the machine;
A being breathing thoughtful breath,
A traveler between life and death;
The reason firm, the temperate will,
Endurance, foresight, strength, and skill;
A perfect woman, nobly planned
To warn, to comfort, and command;
And yet a spirit still, and bright
With something of an angel light.

William Wordsworth

A Lovely Surprise

Life has started all over for me.
The young years of happiness
Have come again in a sweeter form
Than a mother could ever guess.
The love and devotion I gave my child
I thought I could give no other,
But life held a lovely surprise for me--
This year I became a grandmother.

Kay Andrew

Children Do Not Realize

Children do not realize
How deep is mother love, how wise--
They do not fully understand
The goodness of her guiding hand,
And yet she's always held above
The childhood things that children love,
And as they grow the long years through,
That love for her keeps growing, too,
Until they learn the full extent
Of what a mother's love has meant,
The heartaches she's concealed within,
How truly wonderful she's been!
And here's to one beyond compare--
The dearest mother anywhere!

Mary Dawson Hughes

There is none,
In all this cold and hollow world, no fount
Of deep, strong, deathless love, save that within
A mother's heart.

Felicia Hemans

Mother's love grows by giving.

Charles Lamb

Children are the anchors that hold a mother to life.

Sophocles

The Magic of Mothers

There's magic in a mother's touch
And sunshine in her smile.
There's love in everything she does
To make our lives worthwhile.
We can find both hope and courage
Just by looking in her eyes;
Her laughter is a source of joy;
Her words are warm and wise.
There is kindness and compassion
To be found in her embrace,
And we see the light of Heaven
Shining from a mother's face.

Reginald Holmes

To My Mother

They tell us of an Indian tree
    Which howsoe'er the sun and sky
May tempt its boughs to wander free
    And shoot and blossom, wide and high,
Far better loves to bend its arms
    Downward again to that dear earth
From which the life, that fills and warms
    Its grateful being, first had birth.
'Tis thus, though wooed by flattering friends
    And fed with fame (if fame it be),
This heart, my own dear mother, bends,
    With love's true instinct, back to thee!

Thomas Moore

Blessed be the hand that prepares a pleasure for a child, for there is no saying when and where it may bloom forth.

Douglas Jerrold

Mothers' arms are made of tenderness, and sweet sleep blesses the child who lies therein.

Victor Hugo

The mother's heart is the child's schoolroom.

Henry Ward Beecher

Only One Mother

Most of all the other beautiful things in life come by twos and threes, by dozens and hundreds. Plenty of roses, stars, sunsets, rainbows, brothers and sisters, aunts and cousins, but only one mother in the whole world.

Kate Douglas Wiggin

The mother's yearning, that complete type of life in another's life which is the essence of real human love, feels the presence of the cherished child even in the base, degraded man.

George Eliot

Tribute to a Mother

Faith that withstood the shocks of toil and time;
    Hope that defied despair;
    Patience that conquered care;
And loyalty, whose courage was sublime;
The great deep heart that was a home for all--
    Just, eloquent, and strong
    In protest against wrong;
Wide charity, that knew no sin, no fall;
The Spartan spirit that made life so grand,
    Mating poor daily needs
    With high, heroic deeds,
That wrested happiness from Fate's hard hand.

Louisa May Alcott

Memories

The Long Ago

Oh! a wonderful stream is the river of Time,
   As it runs through the realm of tears,
With a faultless rhythm and a musical rhyme,
And a broader sweep and a surge sublime,
   And blends with the ocean of years!

How the winters are drifting like flakes of snow,
   And the summers like buds between,
And the ears in the sheaf--so they come and they go,
On the river's breast, with its ebb and flow,
   As it glides in the shadow and sheen!

There's a magical Isle in the river of Time,
   Where the softest of airs are playing;
There's a cloudless sky and tropical clime,
And a song as sweet as a vesper chime,
   And the Junes with the roses are staying.

And the name of this Isle is Long Ago,
   And we bury our treasures there;
There are brows of beauty, and bosoms of snow,
There are heaps of dust--but we loved them so!
   There are trinkets and tresses of hair.

There are fragments of song that nobody sings,
   And a part of an infant's prayer;
There's a lute unswept, and a harp without strings,
There are broken vows and pieces of rings,
   And the garments she used to wear.

There are hands that are waved when the fairy shore
   By the mirage is lifted in air;
And we sometimes hear through the turbulent roar,
Sweet voices heard in the days gone before,
   When the wind down the river is fair.

Oh! remembered for aye be that blessed Isle,
   All the day of life till night;
When the evening comes with its beautiful smile,
And our eyes are closing to slumber awhile,
   May that greenwood of soul be in sight!

Benjamin F. Taylor

Twilight's Feet

In corridors and caverns of my memory,
I shall run forever along pine-shaded paths,
Wild woodland paths,
    bordering the wilder, lonelier sea!
Forever I'll hear gray sea gulls
Laugh and wheel, rumpling the salt sea air.
Forever I'll sigh when I see the sun
    smile through feather-needled pine trees.
Forever I'll watch the fog mists
Creep through silenced dark,
    slipping among the trees,
    following twilight's feet.
Forever I'll run and feel the splash of rain,
Liquid fingers,
    reaching down to join sad skies and me.

In corridors and caverns of my memory
I shall run forever along pine-shaded paths,
Paths lonely, except that
Twilight in her veil of friendly fog
Runs with me.
Agnes T. Pratt

God gave us our memories so that we might have roses in December.
Sir James M. Barrie

Memory

My mind lets go a thousand things,
Like dates of wars and deaths of kings,
And yet recalls the very hour--
One noon by yonder village tower,
And on the last blue noon in May--
The wind came briskly up this way,
Crisping the brook beside the road;
Then, pausing here, set down its load
Of pine-scents, and shook listlessly
Two petals from that wild-rose tree.
Thomas Bailey Aldrich

The true art of memory is the art of attention.
SAMUEL JOHNSON

As dew to the blossom and bud to the bee, as the scent to the rose are those memories to me.
Amelia B. Welby

Memory

It is an exquisite and beautiful thing in our nature, that, when the heart is touched and softened by some tranquil happiness or affectionate feeling, the memory of the dead comes over it most powerfully and irresistibly. It would seem almost as though our better thoughts and sympathies were charms, in virtue of which the soul is enabled to hold some vague and mysterious intercourse with the spirits of those whom we loved in life.
Charles Dickens

Memory tempers prosperity, mitigates adversity, controls youth, and delights old age.
Lactantius

Often a retrospect delights the mind.
Dante

Imagination

I. The Fountain

Into the sunshine,
   Full of the light,
Leaping and flashing
   From morn till night!

Into the moonlight,
   Whiter than snow,
Waving so flower-like
   When the winds blow!

Into the starlight
   Rushing in spray,
Happy at midnight,
   Happy by day!

Ever in motion,
   Blithesome and cheery,
Still climbing heavenward,
   Never aweary;--

Glad of all weathers,
   Still seeming best,
Upward or downward,
   Motion thy rest;--

Full of a nature
   Nothing can tame,
Changed every moment,
   Ever the same;--

Ceaseless aspiring,
   Ceaseless content,
Darkness or sunshine
   Thy element;--

Glorious fountain!
   Let my heart be
Fresh, changeful, constant,
   Upward, like thee!

James Russell Lowell

IMAGINATION

This is the ship of pearl, which, poets feign,
    Sails the unshadowed main,--
    The venturous bark that flings
On the sweet summer wind its purpled wings
In gulfs enchanted, where the Siren sings,
    And coral reefs lie bare,
Where the cold sea-maids rise to sun their streaming hair.

Its webs of living gauze no more unfurl;
    Wrecked is the ship of pearl!
    And every chambered cell,
Where its dim dreaming life was wont to dwell,
As the frail tenant shaped his growing shell,
    Before thee lies revealed,--
Its irised ceiling rent, its sunless crypt unsealed!

Year after year beheld the silent toil
    That spread his lustrous coil;
    Still, as the spiral grew,
He left the past year's dwelling for the new,
Stole with soft step its shining archway through,
    Built up its idle door,
Stretched in his last-found home, and knew the old no more.

Thanks for the heavenly message brought by thee,
    Child of the wandering sea,
    Cast from her lap, forlorn!
From thy dead lips a clearer note is born
Than ever Triton blew from wreathed horn!
    While on mine ear it rings,
Through the deep caves of thought I hear a voice that sings:--

Build thee more stately mansions, O my soul,
    As the swift seasons roll!
    Leave thy low-vaulted past!
Let each new temple, nobler than the last,
Shut thee from heaven with a dome more vast,
    Till thou at length art free,
Leaving thine outgrown shell by life's unresting sea.

Oliver Wendell Holmes

The butterfly is perfuming
Its wings, in the scent
Of the orchid.

BASHO

Say -- listen --
If you could only take a bath in moonlight!

Hey! Can't you just see yourself
Take a runnin' dive
Inta a pool o' glowin' blue,
Feel it glidin' over you
All aroun' and inta you --

Grab a star -- huh? --
Use it for soap;
Beat it up to bubbles
And white sparklin' foam --
Roll and swash --
    Gee!

I just like to bet
You could wash your soul clean
In moonlight!
John V. A. Weaver

Roadways
Roadways are silver filigree
The wandering soul delights to see
Crocheted through space like
    gossamer bands
Which link his dreams to faraway lands.
From crested peak to far lagoon
They decorate earth in a gay festoon.
By motor, by foot, or uncharted main,
In a limousine or a cindery train,
The lure of the road is ever fresh --
Adventure and glamour weave its mesh.
Margaret Lathrop Law

They can because they think they can.
Virgil

The Possible's slow fuse is lit
By the Imagination.
Emily Dickinson

To me every hour of the day and night is an unspeakably perfect miracle.
Walt Whitman

IMAGINATION

High Flight
Oh, I have slipped the surly bonds of earth,
And danced the skies on laughter-silvered wings;
Sunward I've climbed and joined the tumbling mirth
Of sun-split clouds--and done a hundred things
You have not dreamed of--wheeled and soared and swung
High in the sunlit silence. Hovering there,
I've chased the shouting wind along and flung
My eager craft through footless halls of air.
Up, up the long delirious, burning blue
I've topped the wind-swept heights with easy grace,
Where never lark, or even eagle, flew;
And, while with silent, lifting mind I've trod
The high untrespassed sanctity of space,
Put out my hand, and touched the face of God.
John Gillespie Magee, Jr.

The apron-strings of an American mother are made of India-rubber. Her boy belongs where he is wanted; and his home is wherever the stars and stripes blow over his head.
Harold Lamb

The day becomes more solemn and serene when noon is past: There is a harmony in autumn and a luster in its sky which through the summer is not heard or seen, as if it could not be, as if it had not been.
Percy Bysshe Shelley

Imagination is the eye of the soul.
JOSEPH JOUBERT

Love

Love is the essence of self lost in the being of another.

Mrs. W. M. Gray

The Trinity of Love

In all love there is a love begetting, and a love begotten, and a love proceeding. Which though they are one in essence subsist nevertheless in three several manners. For love is benevolent affection to another: Which is of itself, and by itself relateth to its object. It floweth from itself and resteth in its object. Love proceedeth of necessity from itself, for unless it be of itself it is not Love. Constraint is destructive and opposite to its nature. The Love from which it floweth is the fountain of Love. The Love which streameth from it, is the communication of Love, or Love communicated. The Love which resteth in the object is the Love which streameth to it. So that in all Love, the Trinity is clear. By secret passages without stirring it proceedeth to its object, and is as powerfully present as if it did not proceed at all. The Love that lieth in the bosom of the Lover, being the love that is perceived in the spirit of the Beloved: that is, the same in substance, though in the manner of substance, or subsistence, different. Love in the bosom is the parent of Love, Love in the stream is the effect of Love, Love seen, or dwelling in the object proceedeth from both. Yet are all these, one and the self-same Love: though three Loves.

Thomas Traherne

This is the miracle that happens every time to those who really love: the more they give, the more they possess of that precious nourishing love from which flowers and children have their strength and which could help all human beings if they would take it without doubting.

Rainer Maria Rilke

Perfect Love

Perfect love has this advantage in it, that it leaves the possessor of it nothing farther to desire. There is one object (at least) in which the soul finds absolute content, for which it seeks to live, or dares to die. The heart has, as it were, filled up the moulds of the imagination. The truth of passion keeps pace with and outvies the extravagance of mere language. There are no words so fine, no flattery so soft, that there is not a sentiment beyond them, that it is impossible to express, at the bottom of the heart where true love is. What idle sounds the common phrases, *adorable creature, angel, divinity,* are! What a proud reflection it is to have a feeling answering to all these, rooted in the breast, unalterable, unutterable, to which all other feelings are light and vain! Perfect love reposes on the object of its choice, like the halcyon on the wave; and the air of heaven is around it.

William Hazlitt

Love comforteth like sunshine after rain.

WILLIAM SHAKESPEARE

Bedouin Love-Song

From the Desert I come to thee,
   On a stallion shod with fire;
And the winds are left behind
   In the speed of my desire.
Under thy window I stand,
   And the midnight hears my cry:
I love thee, I love thee!
    With a love that shall not die
     Till the sun grows cold,
     And the stars are old,
     And the leaves of the Judgment
      Book unfold!

Look from thy window, and see
   My passion and my pain!
I lie on the sands below,
   And I faint in thy disdain.
Let the night-winds touch thy brow
   With the heat of my burning sigh,
And melt thee to hear the vow
    Of a love that shall not die
     Till the sun grows cold,
     And the stars are old,
     And the leaves of the Judgment
      Book unfold!

My steps are nightly driven,
   By the fever in my breast,
To hear from thy lattice breathed
   The world that shall give me rest.
Open the door of thy heart,
   And open thy chamber door,
And my kisses shall teach thy lips
    The love that shall fade no more
     Till the sun grows cold,
     And the stars are old,
     And the leaves of the Judgment
      Book unfold!

Bayard Taylor

LOVE

How Do I Love Thee?

How do I love thee? Let me count the ways.
I love thee to the depth and breadth and height
My soul can reach, when feeling out of sight
For the ends of Being and ideal Grace.
I love thee to the level of every day's
Most quiet need, by sun and candlelight.
I love thee freely, as men strive for Right;
I love thee purely, as they turn from Praise.
I love thee with the passion put to use
In my old griefs, and with my childhood's faith.
I love thee with a love I seemed to lose
With my lost saints — I love thee with the breath,
Smiles, tears, of all my life! — and, if God choose,
I shall but love thee better after death.

Elizabeth Barrett Browning

Inscription on a Sundial

Time flies,
Suns rise,
And shadows fall.
Let time go by.
Love is forever
over all.

Give All to Love

Give all to love;
Obey thy heart;
Friends, kindred, days,
Estate, good-fame,
Plans, credit, and the Muse,--
Nothing refuse.

'Tis a brave master;
Let it have scope:
Follow it utterly,
Hope beyond hope:
High and more high
It dives into noon,
With wing unspent,
Untold intent;
But it is a god,
Knows its own path
And the outlets of the sky.
It was never for the mean;
It requireth courage stout,
Souls above doubt,
Valor unbending;
It will reward,--
They shall return
More than they were,
And ever ascending.
Leave all for love;
Yet, hear me, yet,
One word more thy heart behoved,
One pulse more of firm endeavor,--
Keep thee to-day,
To-morrow, forever,
Free as an Arab
Of thy beloved.

Cling with life to the maid;
But when the surprise,
First vague shadow of surmise,
Flits across her bosom young
Of a joy apart from thee,
Free be she, fancy-free;
Nor thou detain her vesture's hem,
Nor the palest rose she flung
From her summer diadem.

Though thou loved her as thyself,
As a self of purer clay,
Though her parting dims the day,
Stealing grace from all alive;
Heartily know,
When half-gods go,
The gods arrive.

Ralph Waldo Emerson

My Love

Eyes seeing,
sounds hearing,
touches feeling,
air breathing
    are you.
Fertile life,
strength beyond,
beauty within,
dedication sacred
    are you.

Eileen Perlman

Contentment

No race can prosper till it learns that there is as much dignity in tilling a field as in writing a poem. It is at the bottom of life we must begin, and not at the top.

Booker T. Washington

CONTENTMENT

A Contented Mind

I weigh not fortune's frown or smile;
   I joy not much in earthly joys;
I seek not state, I heed not style;
   I am not fond of fancy's toys;
I rest so pleased with what I have,
I wish no more, no more I crave.

I quake not at the thunder's crack,
   I tremble not at news of war;
I swoon not at the news of wrack;
   I shrink not at the blazing star;
I fear not loss, I hope not gain;
I envy none, I none disdain.

I see ambition never pleased;
   I see a miser starved in store;
I see gold's dropsy seldom eased;
   I see even Midas grope for more;
I neither want nor yet abound--
Enough's a feast, content is crowned.

I feign not friendship where I hate;
   I fawn not on the great (in show);
I prize, I praise a moderate estate,
   Neither too lofty nor too low;
This, this is all my choice, my cheer--
A mind content, a conscience clear.
              Joshua Sylvester

Contentment

We sit before the fire; how warm inside
And proof against the cold, our cosy room;
The crackling log makes cheery sound; outside
The winter wind roars like the voice of doom.
While burning stars look down and cannot know
How pale they are beside our hearthfire's glow.
              Kay Wissinger

The secret of contentment is the discovery by every man of his own powers and limitations, finding satisfaction in a line of activity which he can do well, plus the wisdom to know that his place, no matter how important or successful he is, never counts very much in the universe. A man may very well be so successful in carving a name for himself in his field that he begins to imagine himself indispensable or omnipotent. He is eaten up by some secret ambition, and then good-bye to all contentment. Sometimes it is more important to discover what one cannot do than what one can do. So much restlessness is due to the fact that a man does not know what he wants, or he wants too many things, or perhaps he wants to be somebody else, to be anybody except himself. The courage of being one's genuine self, of standing alone and of not wanting to be somebody else!
Lin Yutang

Tranquillity:
Walking alone:
Happy alone.
SHIKI

In the garden of life, just think of the flowers
And pass the rest as you go;
Remember the bright and sunshiny hours
And forget the rain and the snow;
Think of the friends who are loyal and true;
Let the rest of the world go its way;
Remember the years, but forget the tears,
And you'll find contentment each day.
Emily R. Gray

CONTENTMENT

I Wandered Lonely as a Cloud
I wandered lonely as a cloud
   That floats on high o'er vales and hills,
When all at once I saw a crowd,
   A host of golden daffodils
Beside the lake, beneath the trees,
Fluttering and dancing in the breeze.
The waves beside them danced; but they
   Out-did the sparkling waves in glee;
A poet could not but be gay
   In such a jocund company:
I gazed--and gazed--but little thought
What wealth the show to me had brought.
For oft, when on my couch I lie
   In vacant or in pensive mood,
They flash upon that inward eye
   Which is the bliss of solitude;
And then my heart with pleasure fills
And dances with the daffodils.
William Wordsworth

...I have learned, in whatsoever state I am, therewith to be content.
Philippians 4:11

That happy state of mind, so rarely possessed, in which we can say, "I have enough," is the highest attainment of philosophy. Happiness consists, not in possessing much, but in being content with what we possess. He who wants little always has enough.
Johann Zimmerman

Great is he who enjoys his earthenware as if it were plate, and not less great is the man to whom all his plate is no more than earthenware.
Robert Leighton

Content can soothe, where'er by fortune placed; can rear a garden in the desert waste.
Henry Kirke White

A contented mind is the greatest blessing a man can enjoy in this world.
Joseph Addison

A mind content both crown and kingdom is.
Robert Greene

Content lodges oftener in cottages than palaces.
Thomas Fuller

Gratitude

Thanks for Everything

For all that God in mercy sends;
For health and children, home and friends,
For comfort in the time of need,
For every kindly word and deed,
For happy thoughts and holy talk,
For guidance in our daily walk,
For everything give thanks!

For beauty in this world of ours,
For verdant grass and lovely flowers,
For song of birds, for hum of bees,
For refreshing summer breeze,
For hill and plain, for streams and wood,
For the great ocean's mighty flood,
For everything give thanks!

For sweet sleep which comes with night,
For the returning morning's light,
For the bright sun that shines on high,
For the stars glittering in the sky,
For these and everything we see,
O Lord, our hearts we lift to Thee.
For everything give thanks!

Helen Isabella Tupper

Gratitude

Be grateful for the kindly friends
   that walk along your way;
Be grateful for the skies of blue
   that smile from day to day;
Be grateful for the health you own,
   the work you find to do,
For round about you there are men
   less fortunate than you.

Be grateful for the growing trees,
   the roses soon to bloom,
The tenderness of kindly hearts
   that shared your days of gloom;
Be grateful for the morning dew,
   the grass beneath your feet,
The soft caresses of your babes
   and all their laughter sweet.

Acquire the grateful habit, learn to see
   how blest you are,
How much there is to gladden life,
   how little life to mar!
And what if rain shall fall to-day
   and you with grief are sad;
Be grateful that you can recall
   the joys that you have had.
Edgar A. Guest

Gratitude is the fairest blossom which springs from the soul, and the heart of man knoweth none more fragrant.
Hosea Ballou

Nothing is more honorable than a grateful heart.
Seneca

Gratitude is not only the memory but the homage of the heart rendered to God for his goodness.
Nathaniel P. Willis

Gratitude is a nice touch of beauty added last of all to the countenance, giving a classic beauty, an angelic loveliness to the character
Theodore Parker

In every thing give thanks.
I THESSALONIANS 5:18

Best of all is it to preserve everything in a pure, still heart, and let there be for every pulse a thanksgiving, and for every breath a song.
Konrad von Gesner

Song

Let my voice ring out and over the earth,
   Through all the grief and strife,
With a golden joy in a silver mirth:
   Thank God for Life!

Let my voice swell out through the great abyss
   To the azure dome above,
With a chord of faith in the harp of bliss:
   Thank God for Life!

Let my voice thrill out beneath and above,
   The whole world through:
O my Love and Life, O my Life and Love,
   Thank God for you!
James Thomson

Gratitude is the memory of the heart.
Jean Baptiste Massieu

We Thank Thee
We thank Thee, Lord, for creating us in Thy holy image and giving us an eternal destiny. We thank Thee, too, for the great abundance of thy blessings on our country—for the beauty all around us, the sea and the sky, the earth and every growing thing. We thank Thee for our many material benefits but more than this, for the gifts of mind, heart and soul which we all possess. The love, truth and happiness that You provide on earth is a foretaste of everlasting joy in Heaven.
James Keller

Thank God every morning when you get up that you have something to do which must be done, whether you like it or not. Being forced to work, and forced to do your best, will breed in you temperance and self-control, diligence and strength of will, cheerfulness and content, and a hundred virtues which the idle will never know.
Charles Kingsley

The Spirit of Gratitude
Our sages said that all things might be lost save one: the spirit of gratitude that is ever present in the heart of man....

The waters of sadness are deep, but they will never extinguish the spark of gratefulness that is fed by man's inherent recognition of God's goodness toward him.

Let us fan that spark into a flame that will guide us happily into the future.
Joseph I. Weiss

Index

Authors, Titles, First Lines

A man must earn his hour of peace 13
A ruddy drop of manly blood 20
ADAMS, JOHN QUINCY 101
ADDISON, JOSEPH 17, 118
AGATHON 50
ALCOTT, AMOS BRONSON 50, 101
ALCOTT, LOUISA MAY 17, 37, 59, 104
ALDRICH, THOMAS BAILEY 106
ALGER, W. R. 20
All day I did the little things 64
ALLEMAN, EMILY CAREY 94
ALLERTON, ELLEN P. 47
AMBROSE, SAINT 72
American Laughter 93
AMIEL, HENRI FREDERIC 26, 34
ANDERSEN, HANS CHRISTIAN 80
ANDREW, KAY 103
AQUINAS, THOMAS 30
ARGOW, W. WALDEMAR W. 42
ARISTOTLE 20
ARMSTRONG, MILDRED BOWERS 58
At Day's End 94
AUGUSTINE, SAINT 25
BACON, FRANCIS 33, 50
BAILEY, PHILIP JAMES 34
BALLOU, HOSEA 120
BALZAC, HONORE DE 45, 59
Barefoot Boy, The 89
BARKS, HERBERT B. 16
BARRIE, SIR JAMES M. 25, 29, 101, 106
BASHO 108
BATES, KATHARINE LEE 13
BAUGHAN, R. J. 16

Be grateful for the kindly friends that
   walk along your way 120
Beautiful faces are those that wear — 47
Beautiful Things 47
Beauty 45
Bedouin Love-Song 113
BEECHER, HENRY WARD 27, 94, 100, 104
Begin the Day With God 29
BENSON, A. C. 44
BERANGER, PIERRE JEAN DE 82
BILLINGS, JOSH 94
BLAKE, THOMAS 29
Blessings on thee, little man 89
Blue Bowl, The 64
BLUMENTHAL, O. 94
BODIN, J. E. 94
BONNARD, ABEL 20
BRIDGES, ROBERT 90
BROCK, DORIS CHALMA 69, 88
BRONTE, EMILY 64
BROOKS, AMY 90
BROOKS, PHILLIPS 71
BROOKS, RICHARD 82
BROWN, WILLIAM GOLDSMITH 101
BROWNE, SIR THOMAS 88
BROWNING, ELIZABETH BARRETT 56, 114
BROWNING, ROBERT 22, 56, 76, 96, 100
BRYAN, WILLIAM JENNINGS 102
BRYANT, WILLIAM CULLEN 69, 85
BULWER-LYTTON, EDWARD 17
BURROUGHS, JOHN 29
BUTLER, SAMUEL 50
By the rude bridge that arched the flood 28
BYRNE, DONN 44
BYRON, GEORGE GORDON, LORD 17, 45, 50, 88
CAMPBELL, JOSEPH 96
Care-Free Youth 63
CARR, MARY BEALE 11
CARVER, GEORGE WASHINGTON 43
CHAMFORT, NICOLAS 94
CHANNING, WILLIAM ELLERY 46
CHEEVER, GEORGE B. 86
CHEKHOV, ANTON 41

Children Do Not Realize 103
Children do not realize 103
CHRISTLIEB, THEODORE 55
CICERO 21, 65
CLARK, THOMAS CURTIS 88
CLEMENT OF ALEXANDRIA 53
COBBE, FRANCES POWER 101
COLERIDGE, SAMUEL TAYLOR 86
Comfort of Friends, The 22
Compensation 11
Concord Hymn 28
Contented Mind, A 116
Contentment 116
COONLEY, LYDIA AVERY 70
COOPER, ANTHONY A. 34
Courage 29
Courage isn't a brilliant dash 29
COWPER, WILLIAM 17, 40
CRAIK, DINAH MARIA MULOCK 19
Credo 58
CUSHMAN, CHARLOTTE 54
CUSHMAN, RALPH SPAULDING 17
DANIEL 2:20, 23 41
DANTE 106
DAVIS, FANNY STEARNS 90
DAVIS, KATHERINE NELSON 99
DELACROIX, EUGENE 56
DESCHAMPS 22
DICKENS, CHARLES 32, 106
DICKINSON, EMILY 25, 58, 109
DONNE, JOHN 96
DRYDEN, JOHN 90
DUPIN, ANDRE 50
ECCLESIASTES 3:1-8 84
ECCLESIASTICUS 6:14-17 22
EDDY, MARY BAKER 23
EDGEWORTH, MARIA 96
ELIOT, GEORGE 37, 104
ELLISTON, GEORGE 81
EMERSON, RALPH WALDO 20, 28, 31, 36, 40,
   44, 94, 114
EMPEDOCLES 56
EPICTETUS 25

EPICURUS 20
ERASMUS 18
Every morning lean thine arms awhile 29
Faith 26
Faith that withstood the shocks of toil and time 104
Father of all! in every age 73
FEATHER, WILLIAM 37, 80
FENELON, FRANCIS DE S. 13
FIELD, EUGENE 21
For a Child 90
For all that God in mercy sends 119
FORD, HENRY 37
FOSDICK, HARRY EMERSON 12, 72
FOSS, SAM WALTER 38
Fountain, The 107
FRANCIS OF ASSISI, SAINT 72
FRANKLIN, BENJAMIN 21, 24
Friendship (CRAIK, DINAH MARIA MULOCK) 19
Friendship (EMERSON, RALPH WALDO) 20
From the Desert I come to thee, 113
FROST, ROBERT 75
FULLER, THOMAS 72, 118
GENESIS 21:6 94
GESNER, KONRAD VON 120
GIBBON, EDWARD 97
GIBRAN, KAHLIL 40, 46
GILKEY, JAMES GORDON 30
Give All to Love 114
Give all to love 114
Glad that I live am I 77
God knew that everybody needs 99
God moves in a mysterious way 40
GOETHE, WOLFGANG VON 17, 28, 34, 45
GOLDSMITH, OLIVER 58
GORE-BOOTH, EVA 90
Gratitude 120
GRAY, EMILY R. 117
GRAY, W. M. (MRS.) 111
GREENE, ROBERT 118
GREGORY NAZIANZEN, SAINT 55
GREGORY OF NYSSA, SAINT 45
GUEST, EDGAR A. 13, 18, 26, 29, 40, 63, 65, 77, 120

HAJEK, LOUISE 68
HALE, EDWARD EVERETT 37
HALE, ROBERT BEVERLY 50
HAWTHORNE, NATHANIEL 17
HAZLITT, WILLIAM 112
HEINE, HEINRICH 84
Helen, thy beauty is to me 45
HEMANS, FELICIA 103
HENRI, ROBERT 50
Her household motions light and free 103
HERBERT, GEORGE 20, 70
HERRICK, ROBERT 72
High Flight 110
HINDI, THE (excerpt) 56
HOLLAND, J. G. 25
HOLMES, OLIVER WENDELL 100, 101, 108
HOLMES, REGINALD 103
Home 65
Home, Sweet Home 62
HOOD, THOMAS 69
Hope is the thing with feathers 58
House Beautiful, The 64
House by the Side of the Road, The 38
How dear to my heart are the scenes of my childhood 91
How Do I Love Thee? 114
How do I love thee? Let me count the ways 114
HOWELLS, WILLIAM DEAN 96
HUBBARD, ELBERT 22
HUGHES, MARY DAWSON 103
HUGHES, THOMAS 21
HUGO, VICTOR 12, 58, 94, 100, 104
HULL, GLENNA 20
HUXLEY, ALDOUS 17
HUXLEY, THOMAS H. 87
HYDE, EDWARD 22
I am Music — oldest of the arts 51
I believe in the flowers,and their glorious indifference to the changes of the morrow 42
I believe in the world and its bigness and splendor 26
I cannot find my way: there is no star 58
I have seen a curious child,who dwelt upon a tract 25

I heard a thousand blended notes 87
I Hope 58
I hope that I shall never tire 58
I learned love that is not troublesome 101
I must go down to the seas again, to the lonely sea and the sky 15
I Never Saw a Moor 25
I never saw a Moor — 25
I think that I shall never see 86
I Wandered Lonely as a Cloud 118
I wandered lonely as a cloud 118
I weigh not fortune's frown or smile 116
If I were hanged on the highest hill 101
In corridors and caverns of my memory 106
In emerald shoes Spring pirouettes 68
INGELOW, JEAN 90
Into the sunshine 107
IRVING, WASHINGTON 32, 82
ISAAK OF SYRIA, SAINT 12
It takes a heap o' livin' in a house t' make it home 65
JAMES 3:17 13
JEFFERSON, THOMAS 20
JERROLD, DOUGLAS 104
JOHNSON, SAMUEL 106
JONES, SAMUEL 56
JOUBERT, JOSEPH 96, 110
Just a Thought 20
KEATS, JOHN 34, 68
KEBLE, JOHN 64
KELLER, JAMES 121
KELLOGG, ELIJAH 66
KIERKEGAARD, SOREN 80
KILMER, JOYCE 86
KINGSLEY, CHARLES 121
KIPLING, RUDYARD 101
KLEE, PAUL 50
KOHN, HAROLD E. 63
KORAN, THE (excerpt) 32
KUDER, BLANCHE BANE 64
LA FONTAINE, JEAN DE 20
LACTANTIUS 106
LAMARTINE, ALPHONSE DE 37

LAMB, CHARLES 82, 103
LAMB, HAROLD 110
LANDOR, WALTER SAVAGE 96
LAO-TSE 32, 82
Laughter, like gay ribbons 94
LAW, MARGARET LATHROP 109
LEIGHTON, ROBERT 41, 118
LESSING, GOTTHOLD EPHRAIM 72
Let my voice ring out and over the earth 120
LEVITICUS 19:18 37
Life 77
Life has started all over for me 103
Life is a gift to be used every day 77
Light Shining Out of Darkness 40
LIN YUTANG 117
LINCOLN, ABRAHAM 56, 101
Lines Written in Early Spring 87
Little Boy Blue 21
Little Song of Life, A 77
Long Ago, The 105
LONGFELLOW, HENRY WADSWORTH 32, 55, 78, 90
Lord, make me an instrument of Your peace 72
LOVE, ADELAIDE 72
Lovely Surprise, A 103
LOWELL, JAMES RUSSELL 77, 90, 102, 107
LUBBOCK, SIR JOHN 17
LUTHER, MARTIN 82
MAC ARTHUR, DOUGLAS 40
MAC DUFF, JOHN 59
MAGEE, JOHN GILLESPIE, JR. 110
Magic of Mothers, The 103
MARSHALL, PETER 45
MASEFIELD, JOHN 15
MASON-MANHEIM, MADELEINE 100
MASSIEU, JEAN BAPTISTE 120
MAUGHAM, W. SOMERSET 82
Memory 106
MICHELANGELO 59
'Mid pleasures and palaces though we may roam 62
MILLER, ALICE DUER 13
Misty 88

MIZNER, ADDISON 22
MONTAIGNE, MICHEL DE 84
MONTGOMERY, ROBERT 64
MOORE, THOMAS 104
MORRIS, WILLIAM 49
MORROW, WILLIAM 34
Mother o' Mine 101
MULOCK, SIR WILLIAM 97
My Creed 40
My creed is: Stars 88
My mind lets go a thousand things 106
Nature Lover's Creed (excerpt) 88
NEHERAI, MEIR BEN ISAAC 55
New Day Dawning 67
NIGHTINGALE, FLORENCE 79
Now 28
Now fades the last long streak of snow 68
NUMBERS 6:24-26 13
O Captain! My Captain! 76
O Captain! my Captain! our fearful trip is done, 76
O the miles that stretch between us 20
Oh! a wonderful stream is the river of Time 105
Oh, I have slipped the surly bonds of earth 110
Oh, the comfort — the inexpressible comfort of feeling safe with a person 19
Oh the men who laughed the American laughter 93
Oh the sheer joy of it! 17
Oh, the Wild Joys of Living! 76
Oh, the wild joys of living! the leaping from rock to rock 76
Old Oaken Bucket, The 91
Only One Mother 104
OTTO, MAX 84
Our world is like an instrument 37
PARKER, LEILANI TYSON 32
PARKER, THEODORE 120
PASCAL, BLAISE 82, 83
PAYNE, JOHN HOWARD 62
Peace (VAN DYKE, HENRY) 13
Peace (GUEST, EDGAR A.) 13

PENN, WILLIAM 22
PERLMAN, EILEEN 114
PESTALOZZI, JOHANN HEINRICH 17
PETERSON, WILFERD A. 60
PETRARCH 20
PHILIPPIANS 4:11 118
PICASSO, PABLO 50
PLINY 61
POE, EDGAR ALLAN 45, 100
POLLOK, ROBERT 70
POPE, ALEXANDER 73, 88
PRATT, AGNES T. 106
PRIOR, MATTHEW 57
PROVERBS 15:13 17
PROVERBS 31:10, 25-31 102
PSALM 46:10 25
Quickly, Summer, safely gather 69
REESE, LIZETTE WOODWORTH 77
Remember Me 51
RENEAU, NELL 67
RICHTER, JEAN PAUL 96
RILKE, RAINER MARIA 112
Roadways 109
Roadways are silver filigree 109
ROBINSON, EDWIN ARLINGTON 58
ROBINSON, KENNETH ALLAN 93
ROOSEVELT, ELEANOR 36
ROSSETTI, CHRISTINA G. 101
RUSKIN, JOHN 66
SANTAYANA, GEORGE 95
SAROYAN, WILLIAM 35
SCHWEITZER, ALBERT 36
Sea Fever 15
SENECA 16, 41, 120
SEYMOUR, PETER 79, 80
SHAKESPEARE, WILLIAM 18, 58, 87, 112
SHAW, HENRY WHEELER 25
She Shall Be Praised 102
She Walks in Beauty 45
She walks in beauty like the night 45
Sheer Joy (excerpt) 17
SHELDON, W. H. 17
SHELLEY, PERCY BYSSHE 88, 110

SHIKI 117
SIDNEY, ALGERNON 56
SMILES, SAMUEL 58
Song 120
SOPHOCLES 103
Spring (HAJEK, LOUISE) 68
Spring (TENNYSON, ALFRED) 68
STEINBECK, JOHN 79
STERNE, LAWRENCE 82
Stopping by Woods on a Snowy Evening 75
STREET, ALFRED B. 84
Summer 69
Summer Creed, A 42
Sweet and low, sweet and low 100
SYLVESTER, JOSHUA 116
TAFT, LORADO 46
TAIGI 97
TALMUD, THE (excerpt) 20, 82
TAYLOR, ANN 100
TAYLOR, BAYARD 113
TAYLOR, BENJAMIN F. 105
TENNYSON, ALFRED 68, 70, 100
THACKERAY, WILLIAM MAKEPEACE 54, 94
Thanks for Everything 119
The Crown of the house is Godliness 64
The little toy dog is covered with dust 21
The mist looks down 88
The mountain wears a mellow mood today 11
The skies are blue and the sun is out
 and the grass is green and soft 63
There are hermit souls that live withdrawn 38
There is beauty in homely things 45
There's magic in a mother's touch 103
I THESSALONIANS 5:18 120
They tell us of an Indian tree 104
They that love beyond the world cannot
 be separated by it 22
THOMSON, JAMES 120
THOREAU, HENRY DAVID 60
To a Waterfowl 85
To Age 96
To each man's life there comes a time supreme 28
To Every Thing There Is a Season 84

To happiness I raise my glass 18
To Helen 45
To Mother (ROSSETTI, CHRISTINA) 101
To Mother (TENNYSON, ALFRED) 100
To Mother (WORDSWORTH, WILLIAM) 103
To My Mother 104
To live as gently as I can 40
Toast to Happiness, A 18
TOLSTOY, LEO 25, 54
TRAHERNE, THOMAS 112
Trees 86
Tribute to a Mother 104
Truth 32
TUPPER, HELEN ISABELLA 119
TWAIN, MARK 96
Twilight's Feet 106
Under a spreading chestnut-tree 78
Universal Prayer, The 73
VAN DYKE, HENRY 13, 29, 64
Vast is the sea— 32
VAUGHAN, HENRY 72
Village Blacksmith, The 78
VIRGIL 109
Voice of Faith, The 25
VOLTAIRE 50
WALLEY, GEORGE D. 90
WASHINGTON, BOOKER T. 115
WEAVER, JOHN V. A. 68, 69, 109
WEBSTER, DANIEL 50
WEISS, JOSEPH I. 121
WELBY, AMELIA B. 106
Welcome, old friend! These many years 96
WESLEY, JOHN 82
What will be the morning's mood— 67
When the Mist Rises 84
When Winter waves his magic wand 70
WHITE, HENRY KIRKE 118
Whither, midst falling dew 85
WHITING, EDWARD 66
WHITMAN, WALT 25, 52, 55, 76, 109
WHITTIER, JOHN GREENLEAF 89
Whose woods these are I think I know 75
Why God Made Mothers 99

WIGGIN, KATE DOUGLAS 104
WILLIS, NATHANIEL P. 120
WILSON, WOODROW 20
Winter 70
WISSINGER, KAY 116
With eager heart and will on fire 13
WOODWORTH, SAMUEL 91
WORDSWORTH, WILLIAM 25, 52, 87, 103, 118
World Harmony 37
WORTMAN, EDITH POWELL 70
WYNNE, MAMIE FOLSOM 37, 51
Your friends shall be the tall wind 90
ZIMMERMAN, JOHANN 118

This book is set in Goudy Old Style, a typeface designed in 1916 by the eminent American type designer Frederic W. Goudy. The decorative initials are Ransom Swash Caps drawn by Will Ransom, friend and associate of Goudy's. All titling is set in Constanze, designed exclusively for Hallmark by Joachim Romann. Printed on Hallmark Eggshell Book paper.

 The designer gratefully acknowledges the assistance of Myron McVay & Philip L. Metzger.